THE
SHIFTING
CREEK

A MEMOIR

Mona Sen

BALBOA.
PRESS
A DIVISION OF HAY HOUSE

Balboa Press books may be ordered through booksellers or by contacting:

Balboa Press
A Division of Hay House
1663 Liberty Drive
Bloomington, IN 47403
www.balboapress.com
1 (877) 407-4847

Because of the dynamic nature of the Internet, any web addresses or links contained in this book may have changed since publication and may no longer be valid. The views expressed in this work are solely those of the author and do not necessarily reflect the views of the publisher, and the publisher hereby disclaims any responsibility for them.

The author of this book does not dispense medical advice or prescribe the use of any technique as a form of treatment for physical, emotional, or medical problems without the advice of a physician, either directly or indirectly. The intent of the author is only to offer information of a general nature to help you in your quest for emotional and spiritual well-being. In the event you use any of the information in this book for yourself, which is your constitutional right, the author and the publisher assume no responsibility for your actions.

Any people depicted in stock imagery provided by Thinkstock are models, and such images are being used for illustrative purposes only. Certain stock imagery © Thinkstock.

Print information available on the last page.

ISBN: 978-1-5043-6510-9 (sc)
ISBN: 978-1-5043-6511-6 (e)

Balboa Press rev. date: 09/12/2016

CONTENTS

PART II
A NEW RELATIONSHIP

PART III
CLARITY AND INSIGHT

Acknowledgements to: David for your love and encouraging me to do this, Pam for editing this and its many incarnations, Mom and Jai for being my family, To my Wells "sisters" for not forgetting me, your love and for helping me to see another world, Kathy for being that spark that helped to ignite the desire to tell my story, Mary my special friend and angel thank you for making life more comfortable and for helping me along this journey.

PREFACE

Home, a sanctuary for many who search
For a balance in states of existing
Chaos that defines the very thread that
Needs to be homespun so as not to break
--Mona Sen

Now that I look back, my fate in life was pretty much determined at age twenty when I was a junior in college.

My family got together for a reunion in New Delhi, India over Christmas break in 1984. I came from college in central New York, where I was a sophomore, and my parents and younger brother Jai came from Jakarta, Indonesia, where my father was working at the time.

After spending time with some family in New Delhi, we went to Agra for a day trip to see some famous Mughal monuments. Mughal history is long but the Mughals, the Muslim dynasty that ruled most of northern India from the early 16th to the mid-18th century, were a stronghold in northern India for more than three hundred years. That day we saw the Taj Mahal, Agra Fort and Fatehpur Sikri--all of them spectacular. What a unique experience to see such splendor of Mughal architecture in a day! The Agra Fort was occupied by the famous Mughal Akbar the Great in the mid 1500's and rebuilt after being in shambles. The exterior of the fort was built in red sandstone, and it became Akbar's military base and residence. I especially remember the parts of the fort that were built in marble by Akbar's grandson, Shah Jahan, who also built the Taj Mahal in memory of his wife, Mumtaz Mahal. The Taj was beautiful -- semi-precious stones in turquoise, jade, mother of pearl, lapis and jasper, all inlaid in white marble. It must have been a chilly day in Agra because in the photograph I have a red shawl tied around my shoulders. I remember how we all felt the cold when everyone had to take off their shoes and walk on the white marble floor before entering the monument; I remember the mountain of shoes of all sizes organized in long lines. The floor was uncomfortably cold until one slipped on those "booties" that were handed out to tourists. As our tour proceeded, young children ran around the structure, touching the cold marble walls with their small, bare hands. The kids tried to step over the pile of shoes, making the chaos worse. The adults just eyed certain shoes with recognition and relief when the tour was over. What made the biggest impression about the Agra Fort, though, was Sheesh Mahal, or glass palace, which was the royal bath and dressing room. The walls and ceiling were covered with small mosaic mirror pieces. With my "booties" on, I stood in a group of people talking among themselves about the beauty of the room we were in. The tour guide stood in the middle of the group and pulled out a matchbox from his satchel. We all watched as he lit a single match. The chatter became a deafening hush as the thousands of mirrored tiles in the ceiling, which we had not been able to see in the dark, each reflected that tiny flame. It was a magical moment. A photograph of the Taj Mahal still hangs in my dining room encased in a simple wooden frame. How easily I traversed the tall marble steps in those days is but a memory. The runaway train called "multiple sclerosis" has changed my life and seems to be beyond anyone's control much of the time. But disability hasn't changed who I am or kept me from living as I choose.

I belong to two worlds, but I think of myself as a person of the whole world. My life in India was many things, none of them easy, but America has challenged me, too. Who I was in India and who I became afterward have been shaped by events and personal growth as I searched for a metaphor to represent what it means to be part Indian and part American. Was my life more like a messy pile of shoes, or was it a single flame magnified by many reflections?

This is a story about an unusual childhood, lots of movement -- several houses in several countries, a relationship with chronic illness, and finally a home and peace. Writing down my experiences and attitudes surrounding the events of my life has clarified in my mind that such happenings may be entirely personal, without the necessity for others to have felt the same way. Like the beautiful Mughal monuments, India means different things to different people, particularly to those of us who were born and raised there. The other part of my heritage, America, allowed me to observe things as a teenager, young adult, and now at fifty, while I could remain as detached or involved as I chose to be. The influence of others in my family shaped me from a very young age, in ways that gave me my character and much of my strength but at the same time were often contradictory and confusing. After many years I have learned that some of these influences were at odds with my nature, and at last I have been able to let go of them and find peace.

Why should my story be any different than anyone else with MS or any disability? We all bear hardships, whatever our circumstances. My interest is in sharing the ways in which I have learned to sort out some of the sense and non-sense. It's a story I live every day, and I expect that will be the case through the rest of my life. I hope that some of the lessons I have learned -- some through trial and error, others through big mistakes, and some by accident -- may be of value to others.

Some people don't stop to look at the picture of the Taj Mahal in my dining room. Perhaps the frame isn't eye-catching enough or the subject is just too unfamiliar. But that picture reminds me that unfamiliarity was a common way of defining my existence for much of my life. People who know me consider my life exotic, unusual, but in retrospect it was --and sometimes still is -- simply an unfamiliar place that I've had to learn to make part of my home, my world, myself.

PART I

MY HOME

"Where thou art, that is home."
--Emily Dickinson

MOTION

. . . .

The "middle" really is a nice place to be, the best of all worlds. The "middle" was a part of my identity crisis growing up. Metaphorically speaking, my father was brown of Asian descent and my mother is white of Scots Irish descent, which puts me in the middle in a nice shade of beige. I never think of myself as "beige" until I sit next to someone under florescent lighting. Libraries, doctor's offices or environments where you have time to notice such things is when I spent time wondering about my ethnicity. The pigments that we all possess are unique but we as people can be so alike. Those forms that require one to identify oneself as being part of one ethnic group or another always puzzled me. Now the "middle is my identity. Not having a "category" to identify me as "Indian-American" instead of "American Indian," defined my existence. Countless hours that went into figuring out why I looked the way I did just to belong somewhere were just that, countless hours that yielded nothing. But people made me self-conscious. Now it all seems such a waste of time. Over the years the discovery is that I am simply a person of the world and no one really cared who I was or how I looked. In America, everyone is from somewhere else and everyone looks different but for some reason in India it did matter who I was and how I looked.

December of 1965, the year of my birth was a joyous occasion for the Sen family because a female birth among my father's siblings was an auspicious event and my youngest uncle graced me with the name "Anuradha", my Indian name. My Bengali family from West Bengal consisted of the typical joint family with blood ties that determined one's title and role in the family. My father's younger sister has two boys and three of his own siblings were boys.

MY UNCLE, "KAKAMONI"

• •

M y "kakamoni" or "father's brother" in Bengali, first called me Anuradha, as I lay there as a newborn, kicking my legs and moving my arms in response to his voice. Kakamoni had polio all his life and was the youngest of my father's siblings; he died in the fall of 2008, after living in the same area of India all his life. He was an artist, a beautiful painter, who used his hand-powered rickshaw to brave the crowded Kolkata streets with his sketchbook. When he was young, he had the arm strength to pull himself along by holding onto pieces of furniture since his legs were not able to move. As he aged he was unable to use his mighty arms to "ambulate" instead he needed to use a wheelchair. This man's spirit was contagious and his prowess exemplary because not being able to walk or have a socially accepted body from the waist down never stopped him. His voice was deep but soft as he tended to his pet parrot "Meethu" in a cage in the small living room. Meethu spoke Bengali and was a mischievous parrot, imitating most people in the house.

The main door in the living room was like a passage into another world. It opened onto the artery and crowded street of Kokata known as Gariahat Road, where poverty was raw and evident as some dead bodies lay in the street. A walk down the same street was famous for its *mishti* stores where one could buy

3

sweets wrapped in silver and gold foil, made of cream, sugar and nuts. Someone in the house would often get some *mishti* to have with evening tea. Kakamoni's eyes had such an intelligent look as they danced and almost disappeared when he laughed. I watched him as a young girl in his *dhoti* or loin cloth tunic as he sat at the lunch table after taking his bath. His hair looked so neat and tidy; he combed it parted slightly but back, not to the side like my father.

Kakamoni had something I didn't, an identity.

Secretly envious of people who felt grounded having lived in the same place, even continent, all their lives is something that made me feel bitter towards my father. My father never settled down peacefully in one place and took the family around the world. My immediate family consisted of my brother Jai, Mom, Baba (my father) and myself and we lived and moved within India, Indonesia and the United States and it was as though none of those places was "home". My birth certificate was stamped by the counsel general of the United States embassy when I was born in Asansol, West Bengal which meant I did belong to a place. Since my age did not allow me to retain memories of Asansol, stories that my parents have told me over the years make the place sound magical, stories about the egg *wallah* who delivered his fresh eggs every morning and the fresh milk. My parent's home was so austere, almost stark with a simple layout. This was mom's new home, married with her new child at age twenty one. Current day Asansol is part of the industrial belt in India and a fast growing city in West Bengal. Education and scholarship are important in Bengali culture in both my birthplace as well as in my extended family.

Growing up was a challenging time and only now my true nature has had a chance to surface, unlike in all those places I lived. Intensity and obsessive compulsive mental "shredding" was almost like an addiction in my younger years, enough that a friend once told me I had obsessive compulsive disorder of the brain. This behavior has served an important function in my life since the early days. Now, shredding of information translates into my own research on topics that interest me, particularly subjects involving health. Thankfully this habit and behavior amounted to something useful. As a person I have an insatiable appetite for reading and learning. The tendency to over-think things and not be able to relax was almost like a defensive mechanism in my environment that fluctuated constantly. As a young child other people's trials became a part of my thoughts like blotting paper since for some reason constant analysis of other people seemed normal to me and not exhausting. This tendency to "dwell" is something my father did and as I did the same thing, my family's daily activities and feelings is where I put my own energy for many years to come. The tendency to be overly sensitive as a young person, caused me to anthropomorphize animal as well as human thoughts, often bordering on wanting to save my family from all things evil so that I wouldn't have to dwell on things that were difficult like my being a little "different" from the other Indian kids. One time, I felt so sorry for some neighborhood kids in my Banjara Hills neighborhood in the southern Indian city of Hyderabad, that I gave away most of my clothes in a humanitarian gesture. When I was a child, I dreamed of being someone with a receipt pad and pen so that I could scribble the item name and price, rip it out and hand it to whoever the customer was. I loved the feeling of being important enough to sign my name onto chits of official looking receipts. It made me feel important, as though the way I wrote the receipt had authority or something. This way I set up shop at my bedroom window and scribbled lots of receipts for lots of kids who showed up in droves. My mother probably wondered what was going on and at some point I had to pay for my humanitarian deed. One time I stole ten rupees from my mother's purse because she had it and I knew where it was. This money which was a lot for my mother in those days bought lots of chocolates in shiny wrapping paper, crinkly and colorful. The poor Indian gentleman who sold me the candy wrote me a receipt which eventually reached my mother's hands as she tried to explain the act of "stealing" to me as well as the humanitarian gesture of giving most of the candy to the kids in the neighborhood. I can still see the little flowered basket on my bicycle which carried all the candy from the humble little stall to my parent's home, bouncing along unpaved streets on the route home. Throughout my life until the age of twenty, excelling at athletics and wanting to be a famous tennis player and "reading" people was a part of my everyday routine. But as I "read" people, they read me too, or at least I thought they did. Maybe people didn't care as much about me as I thought. There were people on the streets of India that stared and others who didn't care. Like anywhere I suppose. What people thought about my presence, bi-racial looks, my intellect, winning a race or just walking down the street was something that concerned me. That seems a lot for someone who should be exploring life, not living everyday wondering what people thought. Interestingly, now that my walking has been affected by multiple sclerosis, it really doesn't matter to me what anybody thinks. My Kakamoni used his hand powered rickshaw to get around and do his business so with this image in my mind I continue to persevere. As I look back at the self-consciousness I felt as a young person before my diagnosis and how it was wasted time, it was unconscious emulation of my father, who felt the same way throughout his life and at a much older age.

MY FATHER, "BABA"

- -

One of my fondest memories of my father is of the time he and I built a ship out of cardboard for one of my class projects. I must have been around seven years old. My memory of that ship was that it was black and red on the steam stack part and had a black exterior and red floor. It was magnificent -- to me it seemed as big as the Titanic! I was amazed that the two of us could have built something so beautiful. I remember his delicate hands taping and cutting parts of the cardboard and helping me paint the ship. Another memory from much later, when I was in college, involved more cutting and taping, this time a paper I had written for one of my classes. He came into my room late at night and woke me up to show me his idea; he had cut part of the paper and taped it onto the end, essentially rearranging the text before the days of the word processor!

I know that while Jai and I were growing up, Baba often seemed under a great deal of stress. He never liked to settle down; as a result, we traveled all over the world. I've always thought that he might have been able to begin a life in America but that India was calling him back home. He also gave me the impression that he would leave a place as a way of escaping to another place. He never associated himself with a particular institution, instead he made his own jobs. I can understand his need to do well; after all, he had a family to support. But the moving around was hard on all of us. Essentially he was married to his work wherever he was. And this was particularly hard on my mother.

It makes me sad to recall that he went from being very active to not being able to figure out what to do once he retired, and then he became ill. When his health started failing in his late seventies, he preferred to stay in the house without going outside for months on end. He had developed aspects of dementia which surfaced if he was not properly medicated. Eventually he received the horrible diagnosis of Lewy Body Dementia (LBD). He fought this valiantly -- refusing to accept the diagnosis, always thinking he had Parkinson's Disease -- but in the end his entire brain was ravaged with the little pink proteins characteristic of LBD.

MY MOTHER, "MOM"

. . . .

Mom went to college in the early sixties and looked for ways to find a better life than the one in her small upstate New York town. She was a stunning beauty, with a remarkable resemblance to Grace Kelly. My father got his first teaching job at Russell Sage College in Troy, New York as a sociology professor. Mom was his student as they courted and carried on secretly until she graduated. My father was considerably older than her, a college professor and intellectual, someone exciting in her small rural background. They married in India after finally finding a priest who accepted that a foreigner was worthy of marrying a Hindu. Meanwhile, she had been excommunicated by her own Christian priest in the United States for marrying a Hindu. This set the stage for everything that happened in her life.

In India my mother had to learn a new language, dress in saris and do all things required to enter a new culture. She was twenty-one and had never left New York State except for the odd family vacation with her relatives, prior to marrying my father. To this day, I wonder if my father really understood the sacrifices she made. In his mind she was with family, learning how to be Indian. She has told me of loneliness and living in a foreign land with ways she tried to understand in her early twenties. I remember a time when we had a flat tire in the middle of a busy street in Hyderabad in southern India. Indian streets were chaotic, unorganized and nothing I would wish anyone to be in the middle of, but she just jumped out, opened the "dickey", or trunk, and pulled out her equipment to deal with the situation. She fearlessly changed the flat tire by tying her sari tightly around her body to prevent any interference as she used her jack to pump the car off the dusty road. She was a foreigner in a country not her own, yet she kept her cool instead of unraveling in these sorts of situations or focusing on the spectacle she had just made of herself.

One day there were sheets of graph paper on the dining room table, which she used to map out house and garden designs. She owned books on the Mughals and their gardening style. She loved the Mughals and could recite copious amounts of information about the dynasty. She drew meticulous scaled drawings of homes and gardens, all of which were visions of paradise in her mind.

Each of my parents seemed like a fish out of water when not in their respective countries. What complicated everything was they were fish out of water in their own countries after living overseas for long periods of time. Mom was a white, blond girl in a sari in India and my father was a foreigner in the United States. To young children this reciprocal way of being can cause confusion for a long time, impacting the delicate balance of life as well as one's own growth. But when either one seemed out of place in their own country it was all the more confusing. I admired my mother tremendously when she lived in India. In my later years my admiration continues, as she tries to find herself in the world now, in her seventies, after India.

My Birthplace--
Asansol, West Bengal

• •

M om brought me back from the hospital in late December of 1965. I recall a particular photograph of her in a beautiful sari draped around her body, covering her head with a small creature in her arms. Standing next to her was my paternal grandmother, Dudi as my cousins and I called her, dressed the same as my mother just in a different sari, beaming with radiance at the arrival of her new granddaughter. My Dudi had been a homeopath all her life and kept all her remedies in a small box in her bedroom. My father never discussed the significance of Dudi's homeopathic thinking, learning from other generations of family or her basic views on health. She came to the rescue of many with her small frame and little pieces of folded white paper in which she put homeopathic remedies, little pellets that were nature's own powerful concoctions. "Tilt your head back," she would say in Bengali as she administered the remedy by gently pouring the sweet tasting medicine down our throats. When I was an infant Dudi went in search of a cow with a calf my age, just so that the milk I consumed came from an understanding mother! She and Kakamoni both had little boxes filled with little vials as each of them held important knowledge regarding

11

homeopathic remedies. Kakamoni also practiced homeopathy and learned from Dudi. My parents stayed in their home in Asansol and then Mom and I moved on to Kolkata to be with Dudi for a few months. Dudi's bed was hard and her feather pillows were even harder. She and two of my cousins would lay down after lunch for a nap in her cluttered room on her hard bed listening to the chatter of people on the streets of Kolkata. The windows had bars on them for security and parting the curtains slightly would result in hearing the street life and letting in the heat, so the curtains were usually pulled. She always read us stories from a Bengali book, *"Thakurmar Choli"* translated to mean grandmother's stories or tales. I remember the book being a light blue etched in a silver calligraphy-like writing in Bengali, my father tongue. It was during this time that my "Annaprasan" took place, a religious Hindu ceremony with priests and relatives. The ceremony was dazzling; the priest wore white with a small turban and color on his forehead. Many members of my extended family were present to watch my Annaprashan or "rice eating" ceremony. I was dressed in a small pink sari, small enough to fit a seven month old, with black eyeliner and a shaved head, all part of the custom as my mother dressed in a silk rust colored sari and held me in her arms. Pictures don't do justice to how young and beautiful my mother was in those days and I am so proud to look at those photographs. Her long blond hair in a French twist with the traditional Indian "bindhi" or red dot on her forehead when she held me as I searched for the nearest toy to put in my mouth. Pictures that I have seen in later years show three of my second cousins and one first cousin, by Indian standards second cousins are considered aunts and uncles. These cousins were old enough to understand the significance of the ceremony. Another cousin the son of my Pishimoni or father's sister, six months my junior also had his Annaprashan at the same time as both our mothers held us during the ceremony. The oldest cousin present was about five to seven years my senior and I usually called my young relatives by their nickname with a suffix that designated them as first or second cousin or brother. Years later I realized that unless one is brought up in Indian culture, the suffixes used to identify relatives can be confusing. There is no personal recollection of this event since I was less than a year old, which is when Annaprashan takes place. My cousins, aunts and uncles watched as the priest blew the Conch, or sea shell. True to ceremony this was the first solid food eaten by me in seven months since this was to start weaning me off non solid food onto solid food before teething. During part of the ceremony, I was presented with a number of items, a pencil, a book, money, something that reminds me of the Tibetan ritual in the search for the new Dalai Lama, where a child claims items that belonged to them in a previous life. During the Annaprashan, by choosing your item you choose your vocation. I chose the book. Everyone in the family was thrilled because Bengalis as a rule value education, and most people in my family are academics and successful professionals.

"DUDI" MY GRANDMOTHER

* *

If we ever left on a trip as a family from Kolkata, Dudi, my paternal grandmother, prayed for our safe journey and summoned each of us into her room as she put her small, delicate hand over each of our heads individually and rhythmically chanted mantras. She was a devout Hindu with a small table in her bedroom, one which had a pantheon of gods--Kali riding a tiger, Lakshmi standing on a lotus and a small brass figure of Lord Ganesh. A memorable time was when she, Kakamoni, Baba and I went to Varanasi in Uttar Pradesh, bordered by New Delhi to the west, in northern India where the Ganges flows. My grandmother came with us to make a pilgrimage. Varanasi is the spiritual center for Hindus much like the Vatican is to Catholics. Hindus come here to bathe in the Ganges and often conduct funeral ceremonies. For Dudi this was a trip of a lifetime. I watched her small framed body descending the long set of steps so she could bathe in the holy river. Every morning at home she would go in search of "Phul" or fragrant flowers to put at the foot of her temple along with sweets so that the Lord Ganesh, the elephant-headed god, could pacify his appetite.

Dudi had a particular schedule every morning. She got up early, washed up and put in her dentures, collected fresh flowers for the gods, making sure her temple was clean and ready for the day. After that she had breakfast with the family and as the matriarch asked many questions of all of us. She made sure we were eating properly, having successful bowel movements, were not suffering too much in the heat. She also issued warnings about the city's power cuts to conserve electricity as she continued to collect important bits of information from everyone. After breakfast she went into her bedroom, lit her incense, sat on her bed with her prayer beads and softly chanted words, the echoes of which I can still hear.

My First Home--
East Lansing, Michigan

• •

We left Kolkata in 1967 and moved to East Lansing for a year when my father was invited as a visiting professor at Michigan State University. Memories of my life revolve around nursery school in East Lansing, geese and sheep (part of a farm of some sort). Snow was in every picture my parents took on their large, important-looking Polaroid. Snow! As foreign to me at that point as speaking English. The television in our new home in university housing served as my language coach, even though my parents spoke English at home. My new snowsuit, given to me by my mother's aunt, was bright yellow with colorful flowers, matching mitts, and a hat. This was quite a change from my pink sari! I remember a photograph of my beautiful mother in a dark green silk sari, her long blond hair up in a French twist, standing in front of a Christmas tree with lights of various colors. In the photo there are presents and a friend from the neighborhood. (In our home, Christmas was never celebrated for religious reasons, but for the lights and the giving of gifts. Even though Dudi was a devout Hindu, Jai and I were never forced to adopt any particular religious affiliation, for which I am grateful. I think that this freedom gave us the ability in our later years to choose or not choose to be involved in spiritual things. As it turns out, we both are spiritualists in a universal sense. I am not sure about Jai, but I have participated in various spiritual occasions with friends and now on my own. As a result, I know what I am comfortable with.) The friend in the photograph was a small boy from an Egyptian family, someone I will probably never see again, whose father, like mine, was involved with the university.

My first English words were uttered when my new Egyptian friend tried to take my bike away from me: "My bike!" I rarely spoke, something that concerned my parents. I continued to remain "reserved," all the while thinking in more than one language at a time.

It might be supposed that this must have been a nice time for my mother (when she wasn't breaking up brawls involving bicycles), since she was "home" again. Actually, though, she didn't really feel as though she belonged anywhere at that point in her life. My father continued to pursue his career. He was comfortable in our new housing, but I don't think he felt "at home" either. Mom was always creative and managed to make each place we lived very inviting and comfortable. She never had much to work with in terms of money or furniture, but she somehow put curtains on the windows and placed carpets in strategic locations. As a child, I used to stare at houses in the neighborhood; from outside, they all looked cozy, illuminated by lamps, curtains drawn. I did the same thing when we lived in India. I craved a secure home -- I had only known temporary dwellings. Even at my young age, I sensed that Mom also wanted her own house, not a transient rental or "assigned" property.

My Second Home--
Hyderabad, India

. . . .

After our time in Michigan, my parents moved us to the Banjara Hills area of Hyderabad in southern India. Many of the homes in Banjara Hills sat on top of hills with dusty roads surrounding the houses. A few shanty areas were inhabited by the poor. That time is a blur in my mind, once again because of my age. I have seen pictures of big outdoor terraces, lots of neutral colors with limestone white-washed homes, simple furniture, and a German shepherd named "Mish," a magnificent-looking dog with greenish gray eyes. I have often wondered what happened to him, whether he had a nice life.

Because I was such a quiet child, my parents resorted to a pediatrician to uncover the mystery behind my thought processes. The doctor gave me a test. Instead of fitting various shaped objects into similar-shaped holes in a large box as I had been instructed to do, I took off the lid, put all the objects in, and put the lid back on. The stunned doctor joked with my parents about my being a "precocious" child; my parents were amused, as if this were only to be expected of me.

Finally, to the amazement and relief of everyone in my household, I not only spoke, but spoke four languages: Bengali,

English, Hindi, and Malayalam (a south Indian language), in that order. These were the languages that surrounded me every day. Some members of the family, including my parents, spoke to me in Bengali and others in English, while the servants spoke a dialect of Malayalam or Hindi. I now attribute being non-verbal in those early days to a case of sensory overload as I tried to understand why multiple languages were used to express the same idea.

My parents had two servants in this house, a gardener and a maid. In one of the photographs, the servants are taking turns holding me, smiling; here I am dressed in a sari and Nepalese hat. To them I was like a toy doll they could dress up in traditional Indian garb -- a small loin cloth (or dhoti) and a kurta (or long tunic). The gardener would carry me on his waist around the large terrace area and hold me up to see the views of the city from a higher vantage point than the one I was used to.

We stayed in Hyderabad, but when I was about four years old we moved to yet another house in Banjara Hills. Groups of gypsies danced in spectacular red clothing with bangles and huge drums, performing in hopes that people would give them alms. Many of the gypsies were hermaphrodites and so were shunned by society; singing and dancing for entertainment was the only way they could make a living. These gypsies made me afraid because I couldn't tell if they were male or female. Some of them had dark shadows on their faces even though they looked a little effeminate.

My feelings during this period were profound for my age. Cultural insights and attitudes weighed heavily on my small shoulders, as did the attitudes of others towards my way of life. Attending Montessori school, where life was peaceful and not threatening, was a big point of difference between me and others. Most families sent their children to traditional schools and expected the academic rigor and discipline that those schools demanded; Montessori school was accepted but not the norm. Maria Montessori's teachings had touched even India, and my experience in that school has followed me throughout my life in many ways, such as manners and learning -- not at all the same as a crash course on how to be polite. In my classroom we all had little pink desks that we carried around to do different activities. Cutting vegetables is something I excelled at, striving with the utmost care to make sure that my cucumbers were cut evenly. The teacher appreciated my concentration on this activity, particularly the cleanup, an important part of Montessori's teaching. To this day I maintain a "clean as you go" attitude when engaging in any project, especially cooking. Most of my endeavors have been successful if I am given positive feedback and the freedom to create my own structure, which was the accepted way in Montessori school, although not in the traditional Indian school I attended when the three years of Montessori were over.

My father also got me a dog, a loyal friend who chose me as his companion. A larger dog, one like Mish, is what I had really wanted, since I missed him so much, but a little dog followed me around during the kennel browsing -- a little Dachshund we adopted and called "Iben." He was a full-sized variety, pedigreed, chocolate colored, with a look of being freshly varnished. Iben forgot his diminutive size as he flew around like a torpedo, even chasing larger dogs into our garden pond. Iben protected my mother from crates and cobras that inhabited the back yard and relentlessly pursued the huge cockroaches that occasionally tormented her. He was the perfect dog.

The house was located in dusty, rocky, dry terrain, almost like parts of the American west. While living there, my mother had to take up driving in order to get me to school every day. When she would go places, Iben often went along, or else he would chase the car until Mom stopped to pick him up. I think he loved motoring more than the rest of us did.

Being able to drive provided Mom with some distraction; her loneliness was evident even to me. My father worked all day and often went on "tour" because his field of specialty was rural electrification. Mom didn't really have any friends except for Mary Banerjea, a British woman married to an Indian. Mom and Mary would go shopping in their saris, fiercely determined to explore the Indian markets. The two of them, both fair with light eyes, were quite a sight in a sea of Indians! The Banerjeas had three children, who integrated into Indian society much better than I did. I am not sure why; perhaps it was because they didn't move around like we did.

After a year, we moved to a third house in Banjara Hills. The family stayed here for five years. We had a nice yard and a carport for the family car, a Standard Herald. This little car had originally been navy but had been in a bad accident involving a big fire, and was painted over in white. The car was cute and sporty looking, but I always wished we had a larger car because my father looked odd and too low to the ground when he drove the Standard Herald. Maybe it was the way he held his neck. He came home from work every day looking like he was riding a magic carpet because the car was so low. Even as a child I remember wondering why his driving was not as good as Mom's or why he looked so strange behind the wheel.

My new best friend, Chitra, lived across the street and, since Iben loved the field on one side of her house, we played there frequently. There was lots of open space, but a strange odor always loomed over that field. Some time earlier, a cow had been electrocuted by a live power line in a rain storm. The pungent smell of the garbage in the corner of the field where the cow died is hard to forget. The cow might have been sifting through the garbage when it was electrocuted. Her wide open eyes and that foul smell will linger in my memory forever. Nevertheless, Chitra and I flew kites in the field as Iben chased the shadows in the hot Indian sun. I loved to climb the neem trees around Chitra's house as well as the tamarind trees, whose sweet and sour fruit offered a nice feast.

My brother Jai was born in this house in 1972. Both my grandmothers, one from Kolkata and the other from upstate New York, came for this special occasion. One grandmother wore a sari and the other wore loose trousers and shirts for the hot climate. They were both proud of their new grandson and communicated their joy using sign language and huge smiles, since neither spoke the other's language.

A pattern of illness followed me, all starting in this house in Hyderabad. One summer when Jai was small, we went to visit my American grandmother in the United States and somehow I acquired scarlet fever during the visit. Rheumatic fever often follows scarlet fever, and that's what happened to me when we returned to India; I developed a painful case of rheumatic fever that most greatly affected the joints of my knees. I remember that everyone else was swimming in the pool at my great-aunt's house when I was in the United States, but I had to stay inside because I felt so miserable.

We soon learned that scarlet fever can be a precursor to rheumatic fever, but neither country wanted to take responsibility for the state I was in. The Indian doctors denied the existence of rheumatic fever in India. I spent the next few months in bed, often carried around the house by my father because the pain in my knees made it impossible to walk. At eight years old, life consisted of lying in a bed in the living room, with no privacy. The living room was centrally located, so that by being there I could crawl over to the dining table and take some part in household activities. Comic books kept me alive at that point, as did King Arthur stories. I wanted a sword that I could brandish around to combat all the evil in my life. My father had a sword made by a local carpenter. It was not as long as I wanted, but it made up for size by its beauty. As I admired the sword and was told of the carpenter's workshop, I realized that carpenters around the world must speak the same language through their craft. A poor carpenter in India, sitting in a shack, has the ability to produce an exquisite piece of art just as his better-paid counterpart in the United States does. I named my sword Excalibur, and it represented all good things to an eight-year-old. This sword, with its unfinished wood work, has stayed with me emotionally for years, helping me through tough times -- including hard times as an adult living with multiple sclerosis.

Our next move was traumatic, particularly since our new residence in Himayatnagar, a south Indian town, was simply a "layover" while we waited for a house in New Delhi, our next destination. The year was 1975, Jai was three and I was nine. During our few months of stay, three important incidents occurred, the first of which I believe changed my life forever. Iben met a tragic death when he was run over by a car. Iben was a country dog, not accustomed to city traffic or crowds. Though I was young, I was old enough to be severely pained by the wretched scene: a bloody animal, most of his bones broken, trying to stand up as we approached him. We later said goodbye to Iben as we buried his majestic, broken, shiny chocolate body in a small grave. He lay in the dirt so limp, an indescribable sight that has camouflaged itself in my brain so that I cannot find it to erase it. Iben had been my best friend.

I also said goodbye to Chitra, my next-best friend, someone I thought would be around forever.

Cerebral malaria was the third event that changed my life. This insidious form of malaria caused hallucinations because of high fever. Most details of that time are beyond recall, but

I remember a horrid, "hollow" feeling, as if none of my organs existed, that lasted for days. Since we were still in the layover place, my father had to tie up all sorts of loose ends before we could move again. Montessori school was over, and this was my year of traditional Indian school. It was not a pleasant experience, because there was no transition between the two types of school. A calming, sweet environment was exchanged for a harsh, strict, disciplinary world as I continued to be sick with malaria. By this time, most of the household furnishings were packed up, ready for shipping. Mom and Mary sat next to me as I lay on my mattress on the floor. My father was spending most of his time with his research assistants, working night and day to make the next move possible. My mother insisted that he come home because I was so sick. To this day I don't know why he didn't listen to her.

We boarded a train to New Delhi, where my father had accepted a new position. Indian railway stations are crowded, noisy, and very chaotic. The train shrieked as we negotiated the platform. Someone carried my limp body on board. We rode in a compartment with two long seats and two overhead bunks. The train was a steam locomotive like the one that Mahatma Gandhi had been thrown off of as a young lawyer during the apartheid movement in South Africa. There was nothing particularly romantic, though, about that long trip from Hyderabad in the south to New Delhi in the north. My father had arranged for a doctor to embark every time the train stopped along the way to give me medication and sometimes a shot of some kind so that my health was properly taken care of. I remember being apathetic and not caring much about the way I felt. The rhythmic swaying of the train helped the monotony of the ride, but that's all it did. People with large cauldrons on the railway platforms mixed tea with milk and sugar for purchase. Passengers were handing out money from the train windows for a cup of hot chai. I badly wanted to enjoy the experience, if only I had felt better. The journey seemed endless.

MY THIRD HOME--
NEW DELHI, INDIA

· ·

We finally arrived in New Delhi to a new house in a new neighborhood. The neighborhood was known as Sarvodaya Enclave, a small suburb of New Delhi, across the street from the famous India Institute of Technology. A few miles down the road was the famous Mughal monument known as the Qutub Minar. Sometimes Baba and I would ride our bicycles to the Qutub with a picnic. I just remember that experience being very hot and not always pleasant because the bike ride was never continuous given the hordes of people. Homes in this neighborhood were well maintained, particularly ones that belonged to professionals such as doctors and lawyers. These homes had nice curtains with nice lights at night with manicured lawns. Our neighbors were Sikhs on one side and a Hindu family on the other, with a smattering of Punjabis, Nepali's, Tibetans, Gujrati's and Bengali's in the rest of the neighborhood. The Punjabis next door had a lot of servants who didn't always appear happy. I remember the first day we were in our new home, the Sikhs next door, father and son washed and hung out their colorful turbans on the clothes line, a weekly ritual as I came to observe. Sikhs in India wear a turban as one of the codes of Sikhism, their religion. Younger male Sikhs wear little turbans since the amount of hair at that point in their life is not long enough to merit the warrior type turban adult males wear. Young Sikh boys in my school had a little "ball" on top of their head wrapped by a small turban. As far as I remember, in addition to not cutting their hair, all Sikhs wore a stainless steel bangle on their wrist known as a "kada". This bangle in addition to the hair was one of the codes that all Sikhs observed. I have seen New York City cab drivers who are Sikh all wearing this bangle. The turban colors were anything from a military green to a hot pink, an accessory that matched their daily clothing, pants and shirts or a traditional "kurta," beautifully. The women in this house were fashionable in their long "salwar" and "kameez" tunics. These tunics were very feminine with a long shirt, often with bead work or embroidered patterns along with pants to match, ones that were free flowing or "tapered." A shawl like draping fabric was thrown around the shoulders in multiple ways to complete the outfit. In Indian homes everyone has servants to cook and clean. Mom never liked the idea of a stranger walking around one's home as if they belonged there. And it was not her nature to order others about, like servants. She would rather make her own coffee or wash her own underwear. This was always a cause for tension between my parents. My father might be a sociologist, a published professional, but he did not appear to understand her cultural bias in employing a servant. She had a difficult time believing that it was all part of Indian culture. In some houses like the Punjabi family's, servants were regularly beaten if they did not comply with or obey the master's wishes. Mom was threatened by many people in her life, particularly colleagues at work, but servants reminded her of slavery. Home was never peaceful. Mom always seemed "on edge" and given my "ink blotting paper" personality, I picked up on stressful vibes. I felt guilty by no fault of my own that Mom was uncomfortable, almost like taking on the world's sorrows but in this case those of my own family. The feeling is hard to describe, but particularly when my parents felt uncomfortable in any way it made me feel terrible. Somehow I wished everyone on earth got along or was at least good natured about it. There were many languages around me and several cultural norms that I had to pay attention to. When I finally started going to a traditional Indian school in my neighborhood I was to begin a real adventure, one different from Hyderabad and Montessori school.

There was a school known as The Mother's International School within walking distance from my home in my new surroundings. The "Mother" (as she was known) was French and settled in Pondicherry on the eastern coast of south India which was a French colony for a long time. Now Pondicherry has French street names and is a serene coastal town and popular tourist destination. The Mother was a disciple of Sri Aurobindo, a nationalist, mystic and spiritual guru with a famous ashram as well as a place named for him, known as Auroville in Pondicherry. The Mother had established The Mother's International School, an English medium school K-12, where all the kids in attendance were of Indian origin. I did and did not fit the traditional view of an Indian student. I did since I was great with languages and could navigate around several dialects prominent in my school but I did not fit the paradigm of tradition because I was a person of mixed heritage. Somehow I managed to fit in and make some friends. In school we attended daily prayer and meetings which included student exposés and recitations. We always bowed to the garlanded portraits of Sri Aurobindo and The Mother since they were both deceased, during morning assembly. Discipline at the school was harsh particularly if one wore sneakers with the winter uniform instead of the required black leather or if one did not complete a particular assignment due. I always wondered if the peace-loving Sri Aurobindo or his French disciple would have engaged in the discipline exhibited at the school. We wore white uniforms in the summer with a signature belt, grey flannel skirts and navy blazers with the school crest in the winter. Students recited various types of readings during the morning assembly. We all lined up outside the assembly hall and funneled in as our line was instructed to do so. The school was spread out over a large circle and red sand was the pathway around the premises. I remember all the classes required a walk to get to and always a scurry to get there in time. The kids in school were rowdy, pushing and shoving their way to get in front of you in line for almost anything, water, buying school supplies or just to get to class.

Delhi summers were extremely hot and humid and the water I brought from home was never enough to drink so I often went to a particular classroom on the opposite side of the campus to stand in a long line, cupping my right hand as the attendant poured water out of a terracotta pot with a ladle into my hand. Mom didn't like my drinking water outside our own house but there was no choice. Malaria symptoms were serious enough to make me feel weak and unmotivated in a new school environment and the stress of my new life was an everyday anxiety. Sitting on our new front lawn without the ability to feel excited or happy scared me since all my energy was being sapped by the malaria, besides the water in Delhi, particularly in our house tasted strange, salty. The water I drank at school was probably unsafe, never boiled but somehow tasted better. I liked sitting on our new front lawn because all things like the salty water, being Anglo-Indian and wretched Hindi essays didn't seem important because if I timed it right, the sun beat down on my back, leaving me with the feeling of such comfort not ever wanting to stop the unending surge of warmth.

Also, the neighbors on one side always made mango and lime pickles, filling my senses with a large amount of spices as the pickles cured in the sun. So, on one side the Punjabi's washed their turbans and on the other the Hindu family from Gujrat made their weekly pickles. As I looked up, the Nepali's walked their Lahasa Apso, a mountain dog from the city of Lahasa in Tibet, although not bred for humid weather the dog managed to strut down the street very happy. In the winter time, the temperatures in Delhi ranged between 35-40 degrees Fahrenheit. The temperature inside the house was the same as the outside since there was no central heating that I knew of in India. Getting up in the morning from under a heavy quilt to plant one's feet on a terazzo floor was the hardest part of the day, particularly to a student who had to go to school.

My Delhi school career lasted from the fifth until the eighth "class" as the Indians referred to grades. The aim was to be a good student in a very difficult school system. Somehow, in spite of my fluent Hindi, school was always threatening. A woman in our neighborhood, a teacher in the school was hired by my father to be my tutor after a whole day of classes when I was weary but given my obedient nature I suffered in silence. The teacher always wore a sari, had a stern look on her face, rarely smiled and walked slowly and thoughtfully down the street in front of my house. She always had an arm load of books which she carried in her left hand. She wasn't the type of person I would willingly say hello to if I saw her walking outside my home. In India there was always a respectful line that a student never crossed with a teacher. For example one would never think of calling them by first name. I would go to my tutor's house every day after school, crossing the dusty roads in our neighborhood and remember her setting up a small table in her crowded bedroom. She had two children who also attended my school but we had little contact during the day.

I never saw their father and always thought that he had somehow been killed although I never thought it appropriate to ask. I still remember the smell in her bedroom where we worked together, musty combined with the smell of her kids, their dirty shoes and outside dust, all rearranged after the latest dust storm. The bars on her bedroom window were rote iron with handmade drapes gathered clumsily which did nothing to make the environment friendly. Ambiance was not important, keeping the heat out in the summertime, was. Math and basic memorization of material were difficult responsibilities for me to manage, as were the periodic examinations. These events were stressful because I cowered when faced with academic competition and pressure. Hindi exams were particularly stressful because of the long essays and readings involved in learning the material. Performance was everything. In retrospect even though I craved the gentle teachings of the Montessori way, later in life that exposure in the Montessori school in Hyderabad set a foundation of discipline for me based on my understanding of the material, not performing for the sake of performance. Also, it became evident that it was important for me to set my own structure. But no one in society willingly listens to the needs of a young student, particularly in Indian society.

My athletic prowess was the crowning glory of my four-year school career, not academics. I played basketball, ran track and was on a gymnastics team. Events with an audience brought about exhilaration and revealed my wanting to be in the limelight. Bouts of shyness over the years must have been a defense mechanism in dealing with my family's nomadic lifestyle because it took years to realize that being shy was not my true nature. I did enjoy being on stage whether in school events like the Bhangra or Punjabi style dance, sports, gymnastics or just in front of an audience.

Academics and sports were part of my day, but then there were the scary events that devastated me such as the one where a sadistic teacher in my school played strip poker with my class based on quizzes of "general knowledge". One day when she engaged in her pathological thrill as the class shook with fear, she got up to speak to a student and the heavy metal ceiling fan fell where she would normally be sitting. I can still see the student, her favorite target, a small boy from southern India with greasy black hair always parted on the side. He looked so obedient with his white shorts pulled up a little high on his waist. The school belt was heavy and even the weight did not pull the shorts down enough since his underwear always looked "scrunched" and outlined underneath the white shorts. The teacher never considered the falling fan as a warning; rather, she continued her classes with a vengeance, only glancing back at the fan and shrugging her shoulders as if to diminish the possibility that the falling fan might have dismembered her entire body. Mom found out about this behavior after I recounted what happened, but there wasn't much she could do based on the insular school system and, after all, she was not Indian. She once came to defend Jai on a disciplinary matter and was unable to do much except seem like a hysterical mother. Walks to school were stressful because some cruel kids called me "Anglo Indian" on a regular basis, a not so nice term for person of mixed heritage. Indian students were regularly brainwashed about the British Raj and how the imperial rulers were a part of India for too long, from 1858-1947. For some reason, the "mix" that I represented might have been foreign enough in everyday life that it created curiosities. There were the neighborhood "perverts" during the walk home from school where an older teenage boy actually grabbed my underdeveloped breasts in broad daylight, after which I had post-traumatic shock for years after. One time a middle-aged man was masturbating in a secluded alley as I walked by, his face ingrained in my memory to this day. I would always walk with my head down, sometimes with a hat so he would never catch my eye. One day he did and I ran as fast as I could and did my best to explain the embarrassing situation to my mother. She sent me off to the resident doctor's house and told me to tell his wife that there was an "exhibitionist" in the alley but, as I think back on that, how would an Indian woman have known what I meant by the word? This doctor's wife was a traditional Indian woman, not someone who spoke fluent English. After telling the doctor's wife what I saw, doing my best to articulate what I saw in Hindi, the man disappeared never to be seen again in the neighborhood. I never let my guard down though, which was fortunate because one time a bull hanging around a nearby field decided to chase me home. The animal may have been provoked by some young kids playing cricket in that field just before I walked by.

But there were some good memories during the walk home to balance out the unpredictable incidents. Once in a while an older man pushed a cart loaded with peanuts and other goodies. The peanuts were always hot as I loaded handfuls of them into the pockets of my crested blazer. They were a nice treat when I shelled them on the walk home. I left a trail of shells behind me to be eaten by resident cows and goats that knew my movements. Since it happened on most days, I felt like the patron saint of animals with a line of goats and cows following me home.

The teenage years were riddled with cultural questions and adolescent confusion swirling in my already confused head. I was now a teenager without friends to hang out with. New Delhi was an adjustment and required getting used to. My only real friends were some relatives around the block who were also cousins. They were fun and I liked going to their house. My cousins' house was not far from my tutor's home and I would stop by sometimes on my way home. Mom enjoyed going there too but my father went on occasion. My most vivid memory from visiting my cousins was the celebration of "holi" one year, the festival of colors. People threw all kinds of color on others including pelt them with water balloons full of colored water or just plain water. What a game that was! I played hide and seek with my cousins and others, throwing balloons from rooftops and smearing their faces with color. One never wore nice clothes on that particular day because anyone anywhere could throw color on you.

According to the Indian system, in the eighth grade I had to choose between "science" and the "humanities". Had divine intervention not saved me, I really don't think I was ready to make this decision. It seemed very early to choose your interest without regard to learning, which changed all the time. That was when my father decided it was time for the next move, to the United States. It was timely because I did not have to endure the Indian school system any more, no more sadistic teachers, neighborhood perverts or uniforms that were hot in summer and cold in winter. Of course I had no idea that introduction into American way of life would be an equally difficult process. Besides, this was my fourth school in fourteen years so what was yet another school? I would miss my life in India but adjustment at this point was not something I thought about. It was just easier to fall into a new life.

MY FORTH HOME--
BROOKLINE, MASSACHUSETTS

. . . .

We moved to Brookline, Massachusetts, a well-known suburb of Boston, and lived on Addington Road. Our two-bedroom apartment was small, but it had nice hardwood floors. Mom did her famous "sanctuary" thing, arranging lots of plants around the furniture so it all looked inviting. We lived on the second floor and had a short climb to get there. We did not have a car and either walked to most places or rode the Boston T, the city subway system. I can still remember the clean air. After New Delhi, this was paradise. Everything in Brookline was so clean, the air was so crisp, and the sidewalks on the main street next to the trolley tracks were so wide. America had a special smell that was nothing like India.

There was no beginning to how things began, they just did. I did not own appropriate clothes or shoes, and I spoke with my version of an Indian accent -- a mixture of American and British. Being thrown into this new environment after spending my entire childhood in the third world was mind-boggling and incredible all at once. I could not relate to anything or anyone. At age fourteen, I really felt lost, without a country, without friends, and without an identity. I didn't feel as though I had a home, the appropriate demeanor, the right accent, school, secure group of friends, a pet or anything that was important to a girl my age. One time I mustered the courage to get my hair trimmed at a local beauty parlor along the main street, which was one of the most frightening experiences for me as a teenager since my self-confidence was not even on the radar in those days. Looking back on that time, I can only wish that I had had wisdom to draw on at a point when everything seemed so foreign. Whatever my dad wanted is what I did; it was just easier that way. Besides, I had no choice.

Jai and I had a small television in our room, and soon this appliance became my good friend. The experience was so different from India, where television shows began in the evening -- here they were on all the time. Besides, we never had our own television in India.

My mother managed to pull things together for herself, although it wasn't easy for her either. She went to graduate school at Simmons College in Boston and received her master's in library and information science. I was so proud of her accomplishment, particularly since she single-handedly negotiated her way through a very difficult curriculum. She pulled out several of her old Pendleton outfits from her Russell Sage college days; they were such "classic" styles they didn't seem out of vogue in the preppy Boston environment.

Every day, I babysat Jai while we waited for our parents to return from work and school. Sometimes it was quite late before they returned. If Mom had a late evening class, my father would go to her school to meet her and bring her back, because the Fenway, where Simmons was located, was not safe at night.

Brookline High was a few blocks from our apartment. I walked that route every day through whatever Mother Nature offered up: snow storms, rain storms, heat, or pleasant sunshine.

There were some beautiful homes in this affluent suburb, many of which were on my school route. Once someone asked me to babysit their daughter in one of those homes. I obliged but was afraid to touch anything or walk around inside, it was so unfamiliar. Babysitting Jai at our apartment or the little Russian girl in the apartment below us was easier.

There were several ethnicities in our neighborhood, as I soon noticed, particularly Jews from other countries. A Jewish person was not in my repertoire of ethnicities that I had encountered thus far in life. The Jewish experience became all too real, though, because I was around it all day long. In my English class, we watched films about the holocaust on television. The main street in Brookline had a Jewish deli with kosher foods as well as a Chinese restaurant, both of which we frequented as a family.

My school basically consisted of Jewish, Irish, some foreign students, and black kids bused in from the inner city. Mike Wallace, the journalist of "Sixty Minutes" fame, had attended this school, as had his colleague Barbara Walters. I did not know of these people until much later, long after I left Brookline and became more familiar with prime-time television.

Now that I knew my new school's location, I had to manage the rest. I attended all the required classes and got to know the ways in which this school was different from my previous schools. Actually, there was little comparison. At first, I always stood up out of respect when a teacher entered the classroom. Finally, one particular teacher gently told me that in America students were not required to stand as they did in India, so I stopped doing that. I also stopped addressing my teachers as Sir or Madam, because that also was not the way. Had I known that all these things would have to be learned, sometimes the hard way, I might have been more worried than I already was. All the books in English class were assigned; I never had a choice in declining to read any of them and it was not my nature to go against authority. I recall that the reading list included such works as *Death Be Not Proud* and *Flowers for Algernon.*

The cafeteria was the scariest building in the school to me because of the cliques and chaos, so I seldom went in. Jocks dominated most of the conversations, popular students were loud and wielded power in the small cafeteria, other students just ate quietly. By English class, my stomach would let out an embarrassing rumble that I couldn't always hide. Kids would laugh at me constantly. Before class, as most kids were either eating or socializing, I was the only person in the hallway waiting for the teacher to open the classroom door. Other students used every precious second before the bell rang to either talk to friends or make out with girlfriends or boyfriends. To me, getting to class early seemed like the least intimidating proposition.

One time on the bus during a field trip, three girls in a clique decided to target me, claiming I was sitting in their seat. Their accusations culminated in their squirting peanut butter all over my brand-new parka. I was greatly upset because Mom and I had had to walk a long way to the store from the T stop to buy this parka. At last I had owned a piece of clothing like everyone else -- but now it was ruined. Fortunately this sort of thing did not happen very often; the teachers liked me enough to make sure I was safe. I had a perfect grade-point average in all my classes for the two years that I was in Brookline. Some of my teachers were my only friends, and the limited words we exchanged meant a great deal.

It was impossible for me to make friends, though, because I always wanted to go home to be safe at the end of the day. I did want friends, but I had no idea how to make them. Insecurity and lack of identity prevented me from "getting over myself" and just being one in the crowd. One girl did befriend me at Brookline

High, and we went ice skating at a rink only a couple of T stops from my house. We also watched movies at a nearby theater. It wasn't something I looked forward to; it was just something to do. Once I got home after, my stomach would be growling, so I'd eat whatever I could find. Since I was eating all sorts of things at odd times, I gained weight.

I remember watching some romantic movie with my family one weekend, and I realized that watching anything sexual around my parents embarrassed me terribly. As I look back on this reaction, I know I must have been horribly confused about sex. Moving around as I had done, I had never even begun to understand or experience sexuality. There were definitely more public displays of affection in this school and country than I had seen in my entire life up to then. One time in a dark hallway at school, a black student told me I had nice eyes. Although it was a compliment, his candor made me uncomfortable. His remark may have been honest or inappropriate, but I did not have the tools to figure any of it out. The students, like him, who were bused in from the inner city tended to be a little more abrasive than I was used to; although they may actually have been nice, they were harder to communicate with. It all felt like another culture to me. As it was, I was looking for simplicity, not another culture to incorporate into the existing collection of cultures to be understood. I never saw that student again, but I never forgot his brazen compliment. After all, a compliment was an unusual occurrence in my world, something that only happened in the movies, the embarrassing ones I ended up watching with my parents.

The second year at Brookline was a little easier than the first. I had gotten to know some of my teachers and had a guidance counselor who was always pleased with my performance. He also liked my manners and the respect that I showed him and all the other teachers. I spent most of my free time in the student lounge around a big table with chairs, a civilized environment where some of the administrative offices were located. Here I could spend time doing homework or making small talk with department secretaries. I could even eat a small snack before class -- thank God I had figured this much out. Given my high grade-point average all the kids thought I was very smart and sometimes asked me questions or wanted to be my lab partner. School work was all I focused on, since social things seemed too difficult to figure out. I took a class in oceanography, something that was never offered in my Indian school, and I loved it. I remember dissecting a sand shark and a frog in biology class and intensely disliking my trigonometry class, but all in all the environment had become more familiar.

I started to take more notice of the neighborhood, which was quite diverse. There was a Chinese family across the street and an Australian family at the end of the block. I even said "hello" to some people during my walks and liked that they said hello back. I enjoyed going to Harvard Square on the T and roaming around the bookstores and the Harvard Coop, which had clothing and other accessories that the preppy Harvard professors and professionals wore. It was fun to wander into coffee shops frequented by all kinds of people, including foreign students. I went to Filenes's Basement where Mom would bargain shop. I was starting to pay attention to the way people dressed, socialized, and had fun. I had no idea how to be like these "beautiful" people, but I could certainly dream.

One evening after my sophomore year of high school, my father sat us all down and said he wanted us to know that we would be moving again. An escape hatch from Brookline High was a nice thought, certainly, but at once I also felt an underlying anger -- we would have to go through adjustment all over again!

This time Baba wanted to get our input and have us tell him how we felt about moving. This came as a complete shock. When was our input ever important? His request further enraged me, but as usual I chose to be obedient rather than angry. The choices presented to us were Iran or Indonesia. Iran was not high on anyone's list, particularly since the United States hostage crisis in Iran was at its peak in those days. My father thought Indonesia seemed like a good option The nightmare of packing up began, as we watched the movers come in and quickly pack all our possessions away -- just an ordinary day for the packing company but anything but ordinary for us. I spent that last night trying to finish homework and look up information about this new part of the world I was about to encounter. I only knew it as the "Ring of Fire" from having studied it in one of my classes: many islands, tropical, with several volcanoes forming a ring. The thought of all that seismic activity was daunting, but that was the least of my worries at this point! We left from Boston's Logan airport with a connection to New York's JFK. Our flight to Indonesia left in the evening (I had begun to notice that most of our international flights departed at night). Off we went, not only to a new school but to a new country, just like the last time.

MY FIFTH HOME--
JAKARTA, INDONESIA

• •

Jakarta, only seven degrees off the equator in western Java, is the capital city of Indonesia, which is the world's largest Muslim nation.. When we first stepped off the plane, jet lagged, we were met by a wall of unforgiving heat and humidity. The air was heavy and the sun was strong. The airport itself was spectacular: large and open with palm trees swaying in the wind.

Jakarta is a polluted city with lots of people, who in general are short and have black hair; to me their features looked oriental on first glance, probably because of the large Chinese population in the city. The people, as all the guidebooks describe, smile a great deal. Smiling, giggling, joking, and smoking clove cigarettes are all national pastimes. Our porter at the airport was a Javanese man, about 35 years old I would guess, who giggled every time my father said anything in textbook Indonesian, making it obvious that he could tell we were new in the country. He nodded and smiled a great deal as he orchestrated the handling of all the suitcases and found our new driver, who had been provided courtesy of the Indonesian government. The porter lit up a clove cigarette as my father pulled out his wallet to pay him. As we parted ways, the young man smiled and wished us "selamat tingal," or "happy stay."

The island nation's laid-back atmosphere is characterized by a term we soon learned after living there, "jam karet," or "rubber time." For the most part the country ran smoothly, but we soon learned not to expect anyone to ever show up at a designated time because most people observed "jam karet." Many times my parents invited people for dinner or just to come for a visit and they either never showed or came at least two hours late. Most people wore watches, but I wondered if they ever looked at them. Maybe they just wore them for show, given the number of Gucci and Rolex watches sold in the large "pasars" or markets. Besides the watches, these markets also offered bootlegged cassettes and knock-off handbags and clothes.

My father was a consultant to the Indonesian government and always had money to spend in a way that had not been the case in India or Brookline. I do not know how much he earned, but clearly the Indonesian government provided well for us. We had a driver, a government car, and nice houses with swimming pools and servants. Mom worked at the Library of Congress office in Jakarta, which was part of the United States Embassy but in a different location, not part of the Embassy compound.

We stayed at the Hotel Indonesia for over a month until our house was ready and, since the school term had already begun, we had to begin classes. I had been eager to leave The Mother's International school in New Delhi, and Brookline High might have turned out all right had I spent enough time there; now here I was in a situation I couldn't even fathom. Both Jai and I attended the Jakarta International School (JIS). There were Muslims in our Indian schools, of course, but the primarily Muslim population of Jakarta was south-east Asian of Malay stock, nothing we had encountered before. The school campus consisted of pleasant outdoor walkways, connecting a series of "modules" which housed classrooms. Palms swayed in the tropical breeze. Our classrooms were all air-conditioned, and the intense heat was always a shock whenever we went from class to class. Many of us frequently had colds and runny noses because of the constant changes from ice-cold classrooms to the equatorial heat outdoors. We brought sweaters to school and wore them in the classroom. What a sight that was! Sometimes on weekend trips my family would travel into the "Puncak," a mountainous region outside Jakarta, where the temperature was a little colder -- everyone dressed as if they were in danger of frostbite, but I can tell you that the classrooms at JIS were much colder than that.

Our school buses were of all sizes, depending on where one lived. The last time I had ridden a school bus was in Brookline when a clique of girls had harassed me and squirted peanut butter on my new jacket. Kids here in Jakarta were not cruel in that way, though; after all, each of us had come from "somewhere else" and spoke the universal language of "internationalism." Going to school was like visiting the United Nations; there were languages and dialects being spoken from all over the world. Parents of JIS students were diplomats, academics, consultants, military and oil company personnel. Many students were mixed-blooded in all combinations -- European, Asian, African, African-American, and all flavors one could imagine. Some students were citizens of countries they had never seen because they had been born elsewhere or their parents traveled continuously. The lifestyle was certainly different from anything else in my experience, but the other kids at school seemed comfortable with this. So, while I should have felt right at home in this sea of lost souls, I didn't -- the feeling of not belonging anywhere seemed greater to me in a country where we were guests. This was neither India nor America. When pressured to identify my ethnic origins, I would claim the United States because that had been my last stop; I got used to people saying, "but you don't look American." Their reaction was a natural one, since I didn't fit the stereotype of what some students thought Americans "should" look like: blond and fair, or a model from *Baywatch*. I began to wonder if running from place to place without a settled feeling was the way life was going to be forever. What made my father not settle in one place? Was he afraid of something? Of course, I will never truly understand his sense of restlessness, but I suspect he never understood my need for a sense of belonging.

My previous school in Brookline was in a pristine suburb where third-world crowds were not an issue and neither was third-world traffic. The Hotel Indonesia was in the center of town, where the characteristic South East Asian traffic and congestion were very evident. In order to catch the large school bus that arrived in front of the Hotel Mandarin, which in the early eighties was on the other side of the traffic circle, opposite the Hotel Indonesia, I had to brave the heat and negotiate early morning traffic. My trek across Jalan Thamrin, the main artery in this city, involved dodging three-wheeled scooters, other buses, skilled pedestrians, and cars of all sizes and shapes. Traffic came off the circle and poured onto the street I had to cross. Fortunately in those days, running fast with my book bag in tow was no challenge for me.

All this excitement occurred before getting to JIS, but once I made it to school, other excitement began. Transition into my junior year was relatively smooth considering the circumstances. JIS was based on the American curriculum as well as the European International Baccalaureate program, but since we were new expatriates in Indonesia, JIS required a semester of Indonesian language and geography so we could educate ourselves about our host country. In this class we had to learn the geography of the islands, the remote tribes inhabiting parts of Indonesia, and the basic do's and don'ts, which included avoiding major cultural *faux pas*: never pat a child on the head, never point, and never frown or scowl. Just like in India and Brookline, my school work and sports were a priority rather than socializing, since this environment was socially the most intimidating I had yet encountered. As time went on, though, I did socialize quite a bit. My need to go home to be safe at the end of the day was different in Jakarta than it had been in New Delhi or Brookline, maybe because I was older and more able to turn my attention to things besides myself. There was little time for soul searching at JIS; the pace was rapid and so was the need to keep up with the changes. In later years I've come to understand that "army brats" go through a similar experience, traveling with parents who have military careers. There were kids at JIS like that, but I soon discovered that my experience was very different from theirs. With so much going on, there was no time to explore who I really was because of the need to keep up with this new "international" culture. I continued to question the meaning of belonging somewhere. Jakarta certainly could never feel like "home" to me.

Sports was an accepted and important part of my life in school just as in New Delhi, especially varsity soccer and running track -- both had become a passion. Athletics helped me communicate and fit in with other students, and this allowed me to make friends. There were girls from Argentina, France, Germany, and Japan among the many ethnicities on my soccer and track teams. If someone didn't speak English, it didn't matter, since we all spoke the rules of the game. I was the quintessential athlete and enjoyed the inner game of challenging myself. My father never made time to come to my sporting events, and that was always hurtful. Actually, neither did my mother. She did come to Jai's theatrical plays in the auditorium; maybe the soccer field was too hot and dusty for her.

I was nearly seventeen at that point. Strange episodes of double vision had begun to make playing soccer difficult. Since my coach often placed me in the goal position, my seeming to see two soccer balls flying at me at once resulted in errors, ones the coach had little patience for and had a very difficult time understanding. He showed his frustration by yelling or kicking dirt up in the air in an intense tantrum.

I tried to do everything normally, but it was hard because my eyes hurt. I remember several drives with our Javanese driver, Hamdani, mainly to and from school, during which the little "warungs," or stores, that we passed along the way were fuzzy and double imaged. Finally I figured out that if I shut one eye, I was able to see a single image. My reasoning was that if I shut out the offending eye there would be no interference with the functioning one. I constructed a home-made eye patch, which helped me to see single images and not double ones. This ingenuity in constructing what I needed in difficult situations was to surface later in my life, both metaphorically and physically, as I continued to face several similar challenges. The eye patch made me look like Captain Cook, without the costume party to go to. Hamdani always sighed and looked at me in the rear-view mirror while driving through Jakarta traffic; he may well have been looking for an explanation for the home-made eye patch. It was difficult to satisfy his curiosity, because to tell him the reason in my broken Indonesian would not be convincing, especially given that this bizarre occurrence was a mystery even to me. I wore my eye patch most of the time because, if I didn't, it was very fatiguing for the brain to constantly deal with two images. My family and I thought it was heat and stress and that time would take care of the double vision. The eye patch was part of my wardrobe for two weeks before my vision returned to normal and I continued on with my life. Like most young people, I assumed that the episode meant nothing serious and could be put behind me. I had no way of knowing, as I laughed at all the cultural *faux pas* I continued to make in Jakarta with the servants and Hamdani, that things were changing inside my body in ways that would someday change my life forever.

We had three servants in the house: a maid, a gardener, and a night watchman. The maid remained in the house all day, washing clothes, cleaning and making meals. The gardener never came inside unless Mom needed him for something, usually a task that required brawn. The night watchman came in the evenings and remained awake through the night; it was his responsibility to guard the house. Hamdani came early in the morning and drove my father to work and later picked us up at school as needed. He was paid overtime for coming on the weekends. The servants and Hamdani became like family, since we depended on them for so much. All the servants considered us family as well and watched out for our well-being. The servants were different in each of the three houses we lived in Jakarta, but they always integrated into our daily activities and schedules. They all took their jobs seriously, waiting for us to come home at the end of the day even though sometimes we returned late, especially if we had after-school activities or late meetings.

Mom and I would giggle when cultural *faux pas* left us feeling silly, as on the frequent occasions when I substituted similar-sounding Indonesian words for others in the wrong context. Words such as "rumput," which means "grass," and "ramput," which means "hair," or "korek api" (match) instead of "kereta api" (train) -- these sorts of confusions made the servants double over in peals of laughter, since most of the time I was unaware of the mistakes I had made! Many a time on my way to get my hair cut I would inform the maid that I was going to get my "grass" cut;

she would manage to hide her amusement in front of me, but I would hear uncontrollable laughter as I left the room.

Once my vision stabilized I played my sports regularly. I came home all sweaty from practice with my cleats flung over my shoulder, still having massive amounts of homework to do. Life was demanding, but I was young enough to absorb the daily toils. Peer pressure in the school was overwhelming, though, and instead of holding my own ground I resorted to following the path of least resistance, giving into attending to popular events and being part of the crowd. One of my girlfriends and I would make plans and go out on the weekends, particularly on Friday nights. We would go to the popular "Block M" shopping area and buy bootleg cassette tapes and knock-off clothes. We would do girlfriend things like get our hair done and go to bars. My schools had all been so different that there was nothing I could share with my best friend except which party to go to or who was popular in school in a given week; the rapid changes in my mind forced me to keep up with momentary events and not dwell on the significance of them. Since my friend loved to flirt, something that wasn't my style, she became popular with all the boys. After graduation, she was off to college in the Midwest, closing the chapter of our two years together in Jakarta, though years later we had one reunion in St. Paul, Minnesota. I did have a special friendship with a JIS student whose father was Indonesian and mother German. He was a kind friend. He disapproved of my wanting to go drinking with classmates and going to dumpy night clubs in Jakarta on weekends and parties and antics that led to my finding a prom date. He always thought I was too good to engage in such activities. Years later, I realize he was right. Although we lost touch after graduation, his decency is something I have wondered about over the years as I stare at the silver friendship band he gave me with its crude carving of the Chinese "yin and yang."

Before graduation, our class had one last "hurrah" on our senior trip to Bali, a dream playground for a young person, where being wild and crazy was encouraged by all the students. The Balinese just went about their business, tolerating all the shenanigans of the teenagers who descended on them from Jakarta International School. We danced in the club where Muslim extremists later shocked the world by making victims of foreign tourists. It is difficult to imagine that a place like Indonesia would ultimately be touched by terrorism; the islands are so beautiful and the existence so exotic.

But we all returned to JIS and graduated after our senior trip. There was so much to think about now, like the next step, which for me was college. The European and Asian students at our school applied to colleges in their own countries and went through different procedures from the ones American students went through. Those administrative differences didn't matter, though, because we all were about to experience a more significant journey, beginning our new lives and having to make our own decisions. Recently I have reconnected with several of my JIS classmates on Facebook and have learned how some of us have faced enormous challenges, most have their own families and others are out there somewhere. We all are in our fifties now, settled in the United States, Europe, Australia, Asia, and other places, living our respective lives.

On one of our United States vacations, my mother and I visited prospective colleges. We went on several campus tours, including the seven sister colleges in New England, the famous women's colleges. Afterward I was left confused as if in a state of disbelief, a mixture of freedom and fear. One of the expatriate families in Jakarta also had a daughter looking at United States colleges. We all tromped around looking for the perfect place. My father did not participate in college touring except for one small college in upstate New York that he visited once. Wells College thus became my choice and destination for the next few years, beginning in 1983.

AURORA, NEW YORK

. . . .

Wells College was like a fairy tale. Set in central New York in a hamlet known as Aurora, it is situated along the shores of Lake Cayuga, New York State's largest finger lake. Cornell University is on the other side of the same lake in Ithaca, half an hour away. In the early eighties Wells was a small (~500 students) private women's college. It has since become co-educational, and many new buildings have been added to the campus. It really was visually spectacular, and it provided tradition, academic excellence, and a sense of community. My first visit there left me breathless. Not only was it lovely, small, and manageable, it was like nothing I had ever seen. The people on campus were caring in a way that seemed genuine without needing to impress or be anything other than who they were.

After being accepted, I came to Wells earlier than the rest of my classmates in order to attend soccer camp. This constituted two weeks of intense physical activity and training to the point of total body fatigue. I enjoyed being there early, settling into my new home before my roommate arrived. It allowed my new-found freedom to develop in a place that felt safe.

My freshman room was in the Main dormitory on campus. The bathroom was down the hall, and the telephone resided in an old-fashioned booth surrounded by fire alarms and doors exiting into staircases. My room even featured an old fireplace adorned with tile-work. Though only for show by then, at one time it must have been used to warm the people living there -- according to tradition this building had been an infirmary. Back then, patients and nurses roamed the halls of Main dorm, the nurses dispensing medication to the ill and dying. According to legend, the campus had been built on Native American burial grounds, which for me added to the atmosphere of restless souls inhabiting my new environment. The truth of these tales was attested to by everyone associated with Wells as well as by the Aurora natives. Apparently all these ghost stories and legends were recorded in the college archives.

A lovely footbridge connected one side of the campus with the rest. Walking over the bridge reminded me of a children's story that I had read and re-read as a child, *The Three Billy Goats Gruff.* The main difference was that trolls and monsters did not live under the Glen Park Bridge -- only ghosts, at least according to the legend.

My family stayed on in Jakarta but this time, unlike all the other times, moving was a happy experience for me. Finally, total responsibility for my actions, decisions, course of study, and friendships made me feel powerful. My nearest blood relative was now my maternal grandmother, who lived a couple of hours away in Delhi, New York. Although she passed away in 1985 before I had finished school, her being nearby for much of my time in college made my parents happy. Before her death, while she was in ill health, my father thought it might be best for my mother to return to her hometown, settle down, and establish roots. My mother complied but carried an enormous chip on her shoulder about that one-sided decision that persists to this day. After all, this was the hometown she had escaped from decades ago by marrying my father and starting an adventure that had not turned out as she had hoped. My mother's life had been difficult; now she was returning to the frying pan, so to speak. My parents bought a home in Delhi, New York, and with the help of others fixed it up and made it a wonderful space. It was a nice place to come to on college vacations. One good memory of those years took place during my Christmas break in 1984. The whole family decided to meet up in Agra, India. We saw the Taj Mahal and decorated a potted plant as a make-believe Christmas tree in the room of our guest house bungalow. After that Christmas my father went back to Indonesia and remained in Jakarta while Mom and Jai settled in to life in Delhi. Jai attended the local high school for two years and I continued my studies at Wells.

It was exciting to be seventeen, full of vigor, and ready to take on the new challenge of college and my new-found home in the Main dorm. College life was different in a women's college from the way things generally were in the co-educational institutions I had heard about and later experienced during my junior semester away. Much to my amazement, my fellow students and I had more of a social life and much more camaraderie as "sisters." We had parties on campus and frequented fraternity parties at Cornell and Hobart colleges. Sometimes we would use the Cornell libraries and socialize afterward in Ithaca. A little red van left regularly from Wells and made stops in Ithaca and the airport there. Some of us would return from Cornell at all hours of the night in the van, quite often loud and drunk after a night of partying. Sometimes we just went into Ithaca to shop or study. Some of us had boyfriends in neighboring colleges. I did not have a steady boyfriend but started dating slowly.

I had some really fun times at Wells: our "junior beer blast," "senior stunt," and our friendly rivalry between odd and even classes. Since my class was due to graduate in 1987, we were part of the odd-line and competed against the even-line class every year in a traditional basketball game. For senior stunt, I imitated a professor on stage while only students were present in the audience. Apparently my performance must have been outstanding, because afterward in the ladies room, my friends carried on about it -- but to our horror, the professor's wife was in one of the stalls and heard the whole story! I was particularly embarrassed because not only was I one of his students but my major, psychology, was his field. Fortunately, he never held it against me. Another time, during a fundraising event, my friend Mary and I "bid" on another professor's Fiat Spider sports car (which we had long admired) and were awarded the prize of getting to drive it around for hours. By the end of the day, we had broken the horn by constantly blowing it.

One time, about eight of us piled into another student's VW bug and drove across the Glen Park Bridge! It is nothing short of a miracle that the bridge didn't collapse -- I'm sure the ghosts under that bridge were praying for our safety. We had no reason to do such a thing but a few beers under our belt and a dare to prove our bravery. On another occasion, we broke into the dining hall and stole food, and once we broke into a professor's office because we couldn't wait another day for exam scores. We took canoes out onto the lake late at night with champagne and *hors d'oeuvres*, sometimes with our boyfriends and sometimes not. We talked about religion, politics, and the state of the world. We socialized with "townies" from Aurora in our small local bar, the Fargo. I played sports, particularly lacrosse and soccer, and did some long-distance running by myself. Every day after classes I ran along the lake; sometimes I would bike. I know that some students felt the need to have more of a life outside Wells, but not me. I just loved my professors, classes, the small environment, and my daily routine. I was on top of the world

Down the hall in my dorm was a room bearing the sign "JA," which stood for "Junior Advisors." These students were juniors who served as floor monitors and counselors to help the new freshman class adjust to college life. I absolutely adored my two junior advisors because they were personable, smart, and caring. Over the year my JA's dealt with roommate issues and various sorts of matters that seemed like life and death at the time. During my senior year at Wells, I played a similar role as Resident Advisor, inspired by the care I had received as a freshman.

My time at Wells pulled together all the things that had been missing in my life: grounding, friendships, independence, and fun. Life seemed simple. As young college students, nothing seemed to matter much, especially not career or "future" issues. Given the small student population, classes were small and intimate, and attention was lavished on every student. The dining hall was the hub of activity. One met up with friends and discussed academics as well as subjects pertaining to life in general. I just loved the camaraderie of my classmates and of the school itself. I remember my time at Wells fondly and never felt so independent or free in my whole life.

I spent a semester at the American University in Washington, D.C., as part of my junior spring semester away from Wells. That semester in Washington was an exciting time for me. I remember running around the neighborhood where the university was located, running between class breaks to my favorite health food store with just enough time to buy and gobble up my favorite yogurt almonds before the next class. I remember joining friends for Ethiopian food in Adams Morgan and happy hours near the Capitol. I also remember not being obsessive about whether or not I had enough time to catch the Metro to meet my classmates for a lecture somewhere in the city. Many times, because I was running late, I'd have to run down a long line of escalator stairs, dodging other passengers to catch the train. One time I literally ran into Tip O'Neil as he came out of the State Department and I came barreling in to meet my class for a lecture. I remember dropping one of my books and standing up to see a large man looking down at me. What a great city this was!

I then returned to Wells, my little home, to be with my friends and compare "semester away" stories. We sat around my room and talked about the faraway and nearby places each of us had gone to. Several of my friends talked about being in Europe and how challenging it was at times. One friend compared the college where she spent her time away as being so different from Wells, where friendships seemed to mean more. I could relate to that part of being away because, even though Washington was a great city, American University lacked the warmth that Wells had. This just confirmed my decision to remain happy to have chosen Wells as my college. It became clear to me as the years went on that Wells was to be one of the high points of my life, teaching me more than academic rigor but also preparing me for what was ahead.

When the "semester away" was over and I returned to Aurora to complete my junior year, the visual problems began again before the Christmas break. The Scholastic Aptitude Test (SAT) was something we all had to complete before graduation, so I accompanied some classmates to Ithaca one frigid morning before the break, sat down for the test, and saw spots and large grey areas clouding my test sheet. The proctor handed out the question sheets as we all sat there ready to begin the test. The spots looked familiar -- they were just like the ones I had experienced during my daily five-mile run around the track in Delhi while visiting Mom and Jai. As I looked at the test sheet, moving my head in different directions to see the typeface of the test, the realization hit that this might be serious, because the accompanying pain was new. At that point the headache had an extra dimension of pain to it, not one that could be identified. It felt "deep" in my skull, with a throbbing that was relentless. Given all the academic stress coupled with the pressure of taking the SAT's, fatigue may have been responsible for all of this, but I reasoned that it was nothing a good night's sleep wouldn't cure. Mom had driven to Wells to meet me so that we could drive back to Delhi together. I had left my room door unlocked for her so she could come in and make herself comfortable. The door was locked when I returned. My friend Mary was with me, and we went outside and started banging on the window. I looked inside to find Mom lying on my bed fast asleep. She was probably a nervous wreck after having driven for about three hours, since driving was something she did not enjoy. The sight made me sad; I wished, as I had so often, that my parents could just relax and enjoy themselves instead of getting all nervous and uptight -- I knew that she had had a beautiful ride through Finger Lakes country. Why couldn't she be awake enough to say hi? I was nursing a horrible headache, had just been through a hideous test, my semester had ended, and my mother was dead to the world in my room on my bed. To a young person, it felt like tragedy.

My father was home for the Christmas holiday and the house looked beautiful. Mom lit her favorite candles, placing them in the living room next to the beautifully lit tree. Still, the pain made me feel too lousy to enjoy much of it, so my father took me to a local ophthalmologist, who conducted a series of tests to determine the problem. The doctor seemed old-fashioned to me because he started mapping everything on graph paper. What about technology? When it came to some aspects of medical testing, 1986 still appeared backward, and this was one of those occasions. He drew lines and circles and, after a half an hour of testing, once I mentioned the word "numbness," he immediately put down his graph paper and pen and told us he wasn't the specialist who could shed any light on my symptoms. Soon after that, a few days before Christmas, we made an appointment with a local neurologist. He turned out to have an undesirable "bedside manner," to say the least, as he put me through several tests, including a spinal tap and Magnetic Resonance Imaging (MRI), and gave us the verdict on Christmas day of 1986.

DELHI, NEW YORK

. . . .

On Christmas day, two days before my twenty-first birthday, my whole body went cold as I listened to the words of the neurologist. He seemed uncaring, as if my case were a routine matter; "multiple sclerosis," he said, without a shred of emotion. How could he say such a thing when my five-mile run that day had been without incident except for some spots in my vision? How could anything be seriously wrong? Actually, at that moment I had no idea what this diagnosis meant. It just sounded serious. Seated in the chair next to the doctor, I immediately started crying, partly because of the cold way he looked at me -- and after all, it *was* Christmas. He called my present condition optic neuritis, a swelling of the optic nerves, which caused the headache and tunnel vision as well as an overlay of gray film that distorted everything I saw. The doctor was a big man with a grey beard, which made him resemble King Henry VIII, and he peered at me through glasses that kept sliding down the bridge of his nose. According to someone who knew him, he loved wine and horses. I suspected that he had never wanted to be a neurologist at all -- wine and horses were surely more enjoyable. On the receiving end of his apathetic bedside manner, I thought of him as a big bully and felt sorry for the horses he rode.

I remember how my friend Mary and I had laughed in our Biology class at Wells because we couldn't even pronounce "multiple sclerosis" and tried to devise ways to say it without stumbling. People call it MS for short, so apparently they have trouble pronouncing it as well. "Exacerbations" was the technical term for attacks, for which the standard treatment back then was steroids -- the ultimate band-aid for nerve injury at the time. The more I took steroids over the years, however, the worse I felt. The medicine may have facilitated healing, but it did nothing for my overall well-being or sense of confidence. You might say that, in my case, it ended up giving the MS the upper hand. Steroids made me angry and moody, not myself at all. I was too young for this -- why this disruption in my life, worse than having the rug pulled out from under me? I had just learned to enjoy life, but now there was this mess to be dealt with.

Distraught, my parents took me to Massachusetts General Hospital in Boston for a second opinion, but the verdict remained unchanged. Steroids were once again prescribed, this time at an even higher dosage, rendering me mentally and emotionally unable to assess my situation. Things seemed hopeless. Twenty-one years old, without a plan, and lost once again, my life seemed unbearable. This time it couldn't be blamed on skipping across the continents and feeling uprooted; my world had collapsed and I didn't know how to fix it.

We converted the guest room upstairs in my parents' house into "Mona's room" or the "sick room." Wells gave me the junior fall semester to work at home to complete required assignments. The vision had to stabilize and all the pain had to go away before my coursework could be completed and sent back to the school so I could start attending classes again. I returned to college with impaired vision and half glasses to help magnify my coursework. I took every day as it came and continued to enjoy school as best as I could. Even though I was on schedule to graduate with my class, my diploma ended up showing the fall of senior year and not summer as the graduation date. Later in my life, by the time history repeated itself, my understanding of the disease process had become much more fine-tuned and I realize, in retrospect, that the side effects of the medication were not worth the price I paid to get better.

Senior year was fun even though my body was being unforgiving. I was upset that the steroids had "bloated" my face and neck and caused a severe case of cystic acne. I stopped playing sports but ran a little, trying to recapture the allure of running by myself along the lake in an attempt to sort things out. I was determined to take advantage of my opportunities before everything had to end.

Graduation from Wells a year later was a sad time for me The day was made memorable by Peter Jennings, the journalist and ABC news anchor, who had been invited for commencement because his wife was an alumna. As he handed out the diplomas, my classmates screamed at an incredibly high pitch when my turn came and I shook his hand to receive my degree. Over the din, he mouthed the words, "they really like you!"

My little nest was being left behind, and there was no place for me to go except my parents' home, which became a refuge from which to think and make plans. A number of my friends from Wells already had jobs, some got married, and others just took life as it came until they eventually found something satisfying. As for me, I was directionless and scared once again, this time burdened with a chronic illness that threatened to prevent me from living a "normal" life. But there had to be a way to find normal things to pursue! Further schooling seemed familiar enough, so that became my next undertaking.

WASHINGTON, D.C.

• •

The year was 1988, a year after my graduation from Wells and enough time to pull myself together -- or so I thought. Washington, D.C., seemed like the right place for me to go, particularly since my semester away from Wells at the American University had been such a success. I had good memories of my American University days, running to my favorite health food store in the summer heat, interning at a small not-for-profit not far from the college and the DuPont Circle Metro stop. I liked everything about that city: the Metro, the ethnic restaurants, the foreign embassies, the museums, the cherry blossoms. I learned that a friend and former roommate from Wells also wanted to move to D.C., so we joined forces and spent the summer looking for a place to live there. I was determined to go to school in D.C., but I did not feel that I had the right contacts or skills to look for employment. No matter what the human cost, I was determined to acquire those skills.

The application process to get into George Washington University wasn't easy, but it had to be done in time for the fall semester. I took the Graduate Record Exams and spent days completing the paperwork, assembling all parts of the application, and submitting the package to the GW School of Education and Human Development by the deadline. The focus of the program was tourism, which seemed like a good fit given my background. Things were tense while I waited to be accepted; the very odd MS symptoms continued, particularly visual issues and muscle weakness, and kept chipping away at my confidence. Regardless, I kept my long-term goal in mind, which was to start a new life. As I figured it, my taking the initiative -- and the fact that I would already be living in D.C., of course -- was almost a guarantee that something would work itself out.

Meanwhile, even before I left home, my father had moved the rest of the family back to Indonesia, leaving me to stay in an empty house with just my possessions and a cot to sleep on. I was so sad that I cried myself to sleep. At that point I felt that I no longer had a home, nor did I know how to start one. So my emotions were jumbled when, in August, my friend drove up to Delhi, New York, all the way from New Jersey. She helped me load the cars, we discussed the route, and headed south. I followed her as we drove continuously for almost seven hours. My friend had a real sense of adventure and took things in stride, something that did not come easily to me -- not at this point anyway. I was too stressed out, almost as though I were on automatic pilot with no real awareness of what was happening. After unloading me in Arlington, Virginia, my friend -- my only contact in Washington -- left to go back home to New Jersey. I felt ungrounded, abandoned.

My new apartment was a lovely two-bedroom unit, something I had always wanted. There was clean white wall-to-wall carpeting throughout, a stacked washer and dryer in a small but cozy kitchen. It was on Route 50, not far from the Pentagon. Anyone who came to visit me from out of state inevitably ended up in the parking lot of the Pentagon. I didn't have many visitors, but a few friends did come to visit. Since I hadn't developed a plan for covering the expense, my father paid the rent for my new place. As in the past, money issues were not something he ever brought up or dealt with, nor did we ever discuss my one day making my own living; thus I was very ill-prepared for independence or life in general. So much was going on inside me that, given my nature, I need time to process these events slowly -- time I didn't have. Instead, in addition to feeling abandoned, I was still traumatized by my diagnosis. I wonder if I had already put myself in a different category, that of a disabled person. I could not imagine myself being anything different from the twenty-three-year-old that I was at the time, but something always weighed heavily on my mind. Life didn't seem so carefree anymore.

Classes in my tourism program at GW had begun. The route to campus from Arlington into D.C. involved a bus ride to the Metro stop and a five-minute ride on the Metro under the Potomac River into Foggy Bottom, the GW stop. August in Washington was hot, humid, and nearly unbearable, but I did not feel the MS-related heat intolerance experienced by about 80% of those with MS, as I do now. Students in my classes were older, mostly Asian or from the Arab Emirates. One day, two male students sitting near me started to converse in Hindi, speculating about my possible ethnic makeup. The two men had thick black hair, were well dressed, and gave the impression of being employed and going to school part-time. One of them mumbled to the other one something about how I did not look "American," a remark I had heard before in Jakarta. Without a moment's hesitation, I responded in Hindi and explained that my father was Indian. Instead of replying, the two men simply looked at each other and pointed their chairs to the front of the classroom. They never so much as glanced at me again. Some time later, the professor informed me that the two men were Arabs and that my openness had probably been more than their culture had taught them to handle.

During the hot summer months, the search for grocery stores turned out to be a scary experience -- getting lost in areas I didn't

Mona Sen

know was the worst possible fate. Familiar streets were the ones
I followed, never exploring alternatives. I recognized that fear --
especially the fear of not being able to manage myself in a crisis --
was dictating my life, but I couldn't stop. As long as compromising
situations were avoided, I reasoned, there was no need to be afraid.
I became insurmountably frightened whenever I felt vulnerable,
particularly if I thought I might have to outrun someone or
walk a long distance. At this point in the progression of the MS,
ambulation was not an issue, but small ongoing symptoms like
blurry vision and weakness in my arms and legs caused me to lose
a great deal of confidence. I felt fragile, off balance, almost as if
I couldn't trust my body. I had learned to accept my limitations
by operating within set guidelines: school, apartment, easiest way
to nearest store, and where to park my car. Clearly I was not the
same person in the same city as in my American University days.
My situation might have benefited from psychotherapy or an MS
support group in the D.C. area, where I might have uncovered
valuable resources and maybe even made friends who were dealing
with a similar life issue. Unfortunately, the thought of doing any
such thing at the time was not even a glimmer in my survival-
oriented life.

In the grey Washington fall, the dull skies made the world
outside look unfriendly through the apartment window blinds.
I was living in a beautiful apartment, but all I saw was the
unwelcoming world beyond its walls. I felt isolated, with nowhere
to go except campus. My mind was unsettled. I seemed to have
forgotten the zeal it took to get here in the first place. What was
I doing here? How could I pursue something new when I wasn't
feeling up to the challenge? So many things didn't feel right.
Anxiety engulfed my whole being, and I never had a hold on
myself in a way that could generate confidence either for myself
or for the people around me. I was on automatic pilot, without

64

a clue as to where the plane was headed. The primary problem, I now realize as I look back on that time, in addition to fears surrounding my health and basic loneliness, was the fact that my heart was never in the venture. I was forcing myself to get out there and do something with my life, to not think about the MS, to ignore the truth that I was pursuing a degree that did not interest me. Just because I had lived in this city before obviously wasn't enough to give me an edge. Friends, family, or anything familiar was what I craved. I suspect that my symptoms scared me enough to render me unable to think of possible solutions. I think I needed a good friend to advise me, but I had chosen to move to a new city and was too afraid of its unknowns -- plus I never thought to look for help.

After a month of living this way, I just could not cope any longer. I decided to pack my car and leave D.C. At 4:30 in the morning, as traffic on the Washington Beltway was just starting to pick up, I left the district before rush hour began. It wasn't until I reached the Pennsylvania Turnpike that I realized what I was doing and that my left foot was numb from clutching my little Volkswagen Fox. There was no thought of turning back. I drove for seven hours all the way up to Delhi, where tenants were renting my parent's house. I knew I was in limbo, with nothing familiar to hold onto.

PART II

A NEW RELATIONSHIP

"Life isn't about finding yourself.
Life is about creating yourself."
--George Bernard Shaw

ACCOMMODATING MS

I now had to accommodate MS into my life as an ever-present entity, something that not only affected me physically but something that put my emotions on a roller coaster. An example of this new reality surfaced when, finally, I was given a neuropsychological test to measure various cognitive or thinking abilities, such as visual-auditory learning, auditory working memory, picture recognition, and attention. The scores from that test made me think someone else must have been sitting in my stead, to have done so poorly! Neurological damage was happening slowly in my brain, affecting things I had always been able to do -- planning, memory for words and being able to retrieve from short term memory -- and making them into something I hardly recognized. While I was taking the tests, I thought these skills seemed to be working fine. The results showed otherwise. Several people have since told me that they can't do those things either, and never were particularly good at them. It's impossible for me to explain, without sounding tactless, that I once could do them much better than I can now, and that I'm frustrated by what feels like inferior performance. Over time, I've learned to compensate somewhat for my losses. For instance, I make picture flowcharts for planning, make word associations to help with remembering words by putting them into context, and create more associations, particularly visual, to help with short-term memory. Fortunately, my verbal fluency and language skills were, and remain, relatively unaffected.

The MS had now become like a new relationship, taking up much time and energy. The way this relationship evolved over the years was odd, because the remissions became fewer and the way I felt at any given moment depended on how I was coping on a particular day. I read extensively on the subject of MS and decided it was important to be inspirational to myself and others. This attitude has kept me going, though even in those early days I understood the ramifications of what was really happening to me. The Washington, D.C., area had not been my home for very long, and I often wonder if things would have been smoother if I hadn't been so immersed in coping with my "new" relationship. But life now felt different to me, and it was a real and constant challenge to keep up with the changes I was experiencing.

When I finally arrived in Delhi, I had nowhere to go and no way to communicate with my parents; they were still getting established in Jakarta and did not yet have a phone. (This was in 1988, a time when cell phones and email were not as pervasive or sophisticated as they've since become.) A close friend of my deceased grandmother willingly took me in. This kind lady, who has since passed away, did everything in her power to help. I finally was able to contact my parents, who must have had a conference regarding my situation. I decided to go back to D.C. to try again, much as I did not want to. The apartment was still there and so was the roommate I had never lived with. Mom made the long voyage to Washington, D.C., from Jakarta to try to get me and my circumstances under control. I met Mom at the airport and could see the fatigue in her step. It was clear she wanted to help, but a mother might not have been what I needed at the time. An objective but helpful friend was what I needed.

My roommate meant well but, being so fresh with new wounds, I needed someone more capable of dealing with my predicament. One evening while my mother and I were sitting in the living room of the Arlington apartment, my heart started racing even though I was not moving. Then the hyperventilating began. It became obvious that this was a panic attack and that if I didn't calm down who knew what might have happened. My mother did her best to calm me down. The anxiety was mounting and I seemed to have no way to deal with it. In retrospect I wonder if steroids contributed to the anxiety. When I think back to what I did next, which was to return to Jakarta with my mother, it puzzles me. Fear prevented me from looking for solutions; it just propelled me on a foggy path to nowhere.

We flew back to Jakarta together, enduring the long trip, jet lag, and everything that comes with international travel. Clearly I just needed to be home, wherever that was at the time. After all my efforts to get into GW, now I had to figure out what to do about it. I didn't miss my classes much; my motivation to stay enrolled wasn't as great as one would have thought. There was leftover course work for GW, which I completed by doing a project on Bali, a quite extensive one that involved a great deal of research. Baba helped me make all the right contacts with Balinese government officials, had his secretary type up my work, and traveled to Bali with me. The idea for the project however, was my mother's. Bali in the late eighties was a popular tourist destination, but parts of the island were relatively untouched by tourism. My guide and companion was an American and a long-time resident of Bali who had taken a Balinese name, I Wayan Budiasa, and converted to Hinduism. He appeared to be a frustrated American who wanted to live the Balinese lifestyle, giving up his former culture. We drove in his jeep around the island, the splendor of which I cannot even begin to describe.

The environment was lush with vegetation, tropical plants, and people either going or returning from temple while balancing huge baskets full of flowers and fruit on their heads. How could anything be so beautiful? The beauty of the Balinese and their version of Hinduism, different from that practiced in India, is particularly riveting, since the little island is surrounded by the world's largest Muslim country, Indonesia.

It seemed as though the Balinese, both young and old, were genetically predisposed to artisanship of various kinds. One time a Balinese painter broke into dance while he painted a picture of two dancers from the famous "Kecak" or monkey dance. This dance, which tourists love to watch, is based on the "Ramayana," the famous Hindu epic about Rama, Sita and Hanuman, the monkey deity. I witnessed all sorts of things in Bali, including the tourism that brought with it money for the Balinese but was also fraught with some not-so-nice things. One time I remember some drunken tourists with a table full of beer cans imitating a Balinese returning from temple with a basket on her head. Except that instead of the basket being full of flowers and temple offerings, it was full of empty beer cans. The clumsy tourists tried to walk with the full basket on their heads the way the Balinese walk along the rice paddies coming home from temple. The basket never stayed on their heads and the tourists kept dropping the cans all over the floor. Finally, a Balinese waitress came over, quietly picked up the cans and, balancing the basket on her head, gracefully walked away. The tourists laughed without shame, oblivious to the disrespect they were showing.

Over the years my project has gotten lost somewhere. Unfortunately, all that hard work and the interviews I did in Bali didn't culminate in anything significant, just a grade. My heart and mind did not seem to be in this project. It was interesting to see the island and to get to know some of the people, but sometimes I felt as though I was just going through the motions, wanting to please my parents rather than myself. Physically, I was dealing with some fatigue, but I was able to navigate and tolerate heat just fine. (Nowadays, heat sensitivity plagues me routinely.) My experiences interviewing various Balinese officials and local people about tourism were interesting and something at which I excelled, but the project was simply not important enough to me to make me want to pursue further schooling.

I moved back to upstate New York with Mom and Jai after a couple of years of living in Jakarta. Because renters still occupied our house in Delhi, we rented a cabin about a ten-minute drive away. The cabin was something out of the fifties -- plaid upholstery, chairs that were noticeably out of date, rooms that were decorated *I Love Lucy* style. Feeling safe with my mother and brother, even though I was not necessarily comfortable not living my own life, was somehow important to me. There was always a feeling of being unsettled, as if we were the world's most experienced nomads. Friends from out of town came to visit and we just existed in a house that was not our own. We stayed there for a couple of months until the family renting our house left for somewhere else.

My mother saw a job advertised in the local newspaper that she thought was perfect for me: it involved working for an arts organization housed in a small church that had been converted into a nonprofit arts center with an office upstairs. I needed something to do, and this was a way to begin to make contacts and gain some work experience. To my way of thinking, a job interview was a formal procedure where one's experience and what one has to offer the employer is questioned while, simultaneously, one learns to interview the employer. When I arrived at the listed address on the morning of the interview, however, it hardly looked like anything formal. I sat in what appeared to be a cane chair, the type one puts on one's porch in the summer. The director, who was in her forties, looked intense to me, a tall wiry woman whose hips were unusually high up on her body. Her face was long, with a strong jawbone. She spoke in a monotone and I couldn't tell whether the voice was coming from her throat or her nose. She was interviewing me in her house, but the actual work site was across the dirt road in the small church. The local NPR station played classical music in the background. There was a woodstove to one side of the room that she put wood into once in a while. The heat was soothing on this chilly upstate New York fall day. Somehow she seemed to be on her best behavior, listening attentively because if I was hired I would be the first employee this tiny organization had ever had. She offered me coffee which I was too nervous to drink but agreed to anyway. While she walked to her kitchen to make the coffee, I looked around, trying to understand the world I had just stepped into. On the walls were some vintage pieces of artwork, mainly little busts of random people as well as colorful pottery and flowers. This kind of art was clearly to her taste, while my taste revolved around more culturally varied paintings and ceramics like the ones I had grown up with, not things I could pick up in a vintage store or on the streets of Manhattan (as she told me she did). I was used to Mughal paintings in India and Balinese crafts from Indonesia. The notion of finding artistry in small things that one picks up -- antiques, vintage or art made from found objects -- was strange to me. The arts world itself was a complete unknown to me. I had never worked with artists before, even though I had been around several artists across the world. I never considered myself 'artsy,' but years later I realized that art comes in many forms and does not have a rigid definition.

After my bizarre interview experience in this "funky" house, I got the position. I had a sense that this new job was to be an unforgettable journey, and indeed it was.

THE LITTLE CHURCH

. . . .

The setting was remote, a little church (known as the West Kortright Centre) turned into a not-for-profit organization, a performing arts center across the street from the house I was interviewed in. This little church boasted audiences who came to see concerts that were usually seen in metropolitan areas at a much higher cost. Here in a country setting the arts seemed really special. All sorts of acquaintances and friends became a part of my life, working at performances behind the ticket table, in the upstairs office, in the little gallery and out on the front lawn. Patrons and second home owners from New York City as well as local audiences filled the church for some world renowned performances during the summer months. Popular offerings, including blues, rockabilly, children's theater arts programs and chamber music drew audiences primarily because of the well-known performers. The director of this small arts center did such a wonderful job at bringing wonderful performers to our area. Along with wonderful performances came moody and eccentric artists. Mood swings and inconsequential details before a performance drove sound technicians and staff mad. It really was being able to meet all kinds of people from different countries, religions and performance backgrounds that made me thrive in this environment. Personal introductions of both artist and audience members was something I really enjoyed like an Irish flutist who found me at the ticket table after numerous long distance phone discussions, during one of the intermissions or the mother of a handicapped child who asked for me personally after we spoke on the phone. The Irish flutist spoke to me a few times regarding travel to our area and also about his art. He has a soft voice so I was just captivated that a performer could be so communicative about things other than his occupation. The flutist seemed so humble and down to earth in our communication that I looked forward to meeting him. The mother of the handicapped child just wanted her son to see a concert but had questions regarding accessibility. I had a personal interest in disability and answered her queries to the best of my ability. I was touched by her affection for her son and the fact that he was so young. The five years at the performing arts center turned out to be extraordinarily challenging. On the weekends, I worked into the night at regular performances or gala events.

The director and I did not agree on most things but she had a uniquely insensitive way of being sensitive. Misunderstandings often happened in this highly charged, egocentric environment, so when she got frustrated she could be mean when she probably did not mean it. Tempers flew and words were exchanged by artists, staff and technical personnel because of moodiness and the artistic temperament. The director understood that I had MS but at the time very little disability if any was evident, so she probably could not understand my confusion or the way I did things. She once gave me a beautiful dark green scarf that she bought me as a Christmas present, something I have never forgotten and invited me to several holiday parties. I have not forgotten about these thoughtful gestures over the years. I worked and did well if I received acknowledgement of my efforts. Sometimes I found it hard to understand what was being expected of me and part of this may have been a lack of experience, I don't know. As time went on and I talked with my peers in other jobs, I got the distinct feeling that I would have grown into any job like most of them, but I was being distracted by extraneous MS issues. After a day of working there, it was nice to come home. Home was where I found relief. I could sit in the den of the Delhi house and just stare at the beautiful garden, dreaming of how "homey" I felt. My friends in other places always wondered how a job like the one I had at the performing arts center could be stressful, since on occasion I had expressed my chagrin at not understanding my duties there. I thought that my duties in my new position were clear and I saw no need to take things beyond the job description. What I did not understand was that the nature of the job and the non-profit arts center way was different from a normal nine-to-five job description. Many more sacrifices had to be made and one was never 'on the clock'. This was a foreign concept to me irrespective of the MS, since one was compensated for one's time in most jobs without a 'labor of love' attitude. This was one of the main reasons the director and I had a difficult time understanding each other, too much was being expected of me and I saw no reason to allow it or maybe I would have had I been able to. I am sure that I would have adapted to whatever was being asked of me, it is that I could not do that. The issue became the demanding nature of that type of work, that is work beyond the job description and my ability to do it, beyond what the Department of Labor coined "essential functions of the job". I knew the director did some work at home probably above and beyond what was expected and did not come to the office until late morning. Personally, I felt like I was being pushed beyond my limits, maybe she did not think so, how could she when I was 26, young and seemingly alright. The arts organization was her life but for me it was just a job. I attempted to do well which was getting more difficult as time went on. Working, in my mind, required discipline and a regular schedule which I have since learned was crucial to my functioning given slow changes in thinking skills. Things that had to be done at certain times were done, such as mass mailings or mailing of the season program. I was not in a position to give 'things that came up' my all since I needed most of my physical and mental energy to function. Things were starting to line up so that it was evident that the way I had always done things was beginning to change, both physically and mentally. Since I was the organization's first employee, I learned as much about them as they did about me.

At one event, the voluntary board of directors was instrumental in the annual spring cleaning of the grounds and the crystal chandeliers in the little auditorium where concerts were held. Everyone was participating at a certain task such as cleaning of the bathrooms, cleaning the kitchen, upstairs office and the small gallery where different mediums of art were displayed during the summer season. Volunteers and staff members participated in the daily running of the organization and looking back this was difficult for me to participate in comfortably because small signs of the MS were starting to become noticeable to me. It was hard to pick up furniture and walk without constantly stopping, my vision continued to blur and I felt very weak when I got hot. Thinking "on my feet" was impossible if I had to spend my energy thinking about whether or not I could manage reaching up high to clean corners. I had to "pre-think" several steps that others took for granted. For example, I found myself visualizing movements in my mind, almost like a rehearsal to see if something was achievable. The unhelpful part of doing that was overcoming my own stubbornness because most times I would proceed whether or not the mental rehearsal was successful. When I did this, I would pay for it in the end because I had not yet figured out how to conserve energy. The reason for not planning my energy expenditure was because I had simply refused to think anything was wrong or that I couldn't fix it.

The heat was starting to affect me physically and my disability had started to consume me in a way that manifested itself in a series of what I call immature incidents. In retrospect they were not 'immature', just that the handling of them took years to finesse since I had to realize that fighting myself was not useful. One day while attempting to complete a project that I had been working on, something set me off and in my fury and confusion I told the director that it was taking more time than usual because of my MS. It was at that point I realized how nobody understood what was happening to me, including me. I was starting to "blame" mistakes and anything that didn't seem right on the MS--despair and confusion must have led me to that. Children who were part of a theater project were running around distracting me and making noise, which added to the interruptions. Children everywhere act this way and I knew it but could not understand why distractions were causing all sorts of anxiety. The impetus was to lash out and blame small mistakes and even bigger ones, such as accounting errors after a performance, on the MS. Seven years after diagnosis, three years into my new job, things were starting to become apparent when I would trip noticeably or drop things, and I had tremor in my hands to the point where I used small wrist weights to stop the shaking in my limbs. The upstairs office in the church was very hot in the summertime and before realizing that the heat was a factor that affected most people with MS, I started to have emotional 'melt downs' periodically when I was too hot. To deal with fatigue, the new symptom, daily power naps had to be introduced. The feeling was odd, lying in an office environment on a small cot with life going on around me but I was so tired at certain times that being "horizontal" was my only focus. Taking a break seemed like such interference, but not doing so had disastrous results. One time without the heat being a factor I started crying with no valid reason to the outside world, the upset was intense but I couldn't articulate my feelings or why I was emotional. Years later I have learned through my own research that people with MS have a very hard time controlling their emotions. This may have been the beginning of this symptom exacerbated by the amount of stress that kept making everything worse. Empathy is what I looked for. Was I using the MS as an excuse? I had no idea. The misunderstanding of it being an excuse has grave consequences, particularly when one's integrity is being questioned. Being pathetic was not something I wanted to be viewed as and the way things were going I felt the need to constantly fight mistakes. Many folks with MS have left their jobs because of the inability to rationally explain changes in one's thinking or cognitive involvement that caused their mistakes, mainly because they themselves don't understand what happened. Sadly, in families such occurrences often lead to divorce.

In spite of the rough spells, there were some people, members of the arts organization who knew others with my condition and provided a source of comfort. One of the regular audience members did the annual MS Walk to raise funds for MS research. She and her friend knew of a lady locally who was much more "involved" and further along with disability than I was. The two ladies and I talked on occasion about some of the unseen things I was experiencing. One time the photographer for the organization introduced me to "Reiki", a soothing, noninvasive healing modality with origins in Japan. This form of healing touch helped me to relax and meditate on my deep concerns. She would not accept any money for her kindness in coming to the house on the weekends to do Reiki for me.

At that point I was walking the line where ability and disability were almost even, just that my disability was not apparent to others. One winter, the beautiful valley setting where the Church sat at the crossroads of four country roads became a winter wonderland but required shoveling to get into the building. Since there were only two of us who worked there, it was up to me to shovel my way into the facility since the other person wasn't there yet. The effort of shoveling was not the issue, as mounds of snow were removed. It was an intense weakness that came over me, one that was different from being out shape. Feelings of anger and frustration in that lonely environment with no one to talk to at the start of my day were confusing. It was at that point that I realized the importance of finding others who understood MS. It became important for me to seek out others with this condition looking for friendships and understanding. Other folks with MS gave me a "group" and a feeling of belonging. I got angry when someone acted insensitively towards me, because to them I was fine. Learning to understand others' perceptions of you--and how sometimes it didn't matter --took years to accept, going back to my childhood. Now the issue was more than identity, it was disability that shaped one's identity. Five years at the arts organization flew by, from age twenty-six until thirty-one. It was difficult to be in such isolation in a beautiful, tranquil setting at such a young age when I needed people who understood, not just my own company. There was a world outside of this rural area that I might have pursued, but the recent feelings made me afraid.

The American with Disabilities Act was not as big a deal in workplaces then as now. Had I known what to ask for back then, I would have. However, I have to keep in mind that had the arts organization been aware of my disability, they may not have hired me. So, it was my merits that helped acquire this job, a difficult thing to remember given everything that was going on. Also, it is not easy to ask for things you need, such as not attempting an activity on a certain day because of the way you feel; in most jobs this is not acceptable. All this was too difficult to sort out since I was feeling things but no one could "see" what I was feeling. In the early nineties, accommodations for people who needed help in the job environment was not the norm, even if it was, I don't think I would have known what to ask for since things that happened to me were inconsistent. The Washington D.C experience was enough to make me not want to try anything for a while. This was fine, but wanting to strive higher was important for my own sense of accomplishment. Interestingly, all the difficult situations that presented themselves later turned out to be learning experiences, all added to my arsenal of wisdom as the years went on.

In 1993 I met someone at the arts center during an ordinary work day when the board of director's hired someone to build a new stage and lighting grid. I did not know that my life was about to change in ways I could have never predicted.

DAVID, MY UNCONDITIONAL LOVE

• •

O ne morning after arriving at work at the performing arts center, I saw that there were some different-looking vehicles outside the Church, containing construction-type supplies. The valley setting that I was used to suddenly seemed small with at least three large pick-up trucks parked in front of the building. So, in addition to my vehicle and the director's, there were more cars than usual. The small auditorium was bustling with activity. It was exciting to see someone else there besides myself and the director. There were tools, men, ladders and chatter surrounding a project about to take shape. One of the board members was speaking with the crew about the details. On the small stage, large pieces of paper were spread out while one of the men pointed to parts of the drawing, explaining the contents to the board member who was also an architect. The man talking to the architect and crew looked familiar to me because I was sure we had met before in a different setting, a performance of some kind. As he looked at me and smiled, I knew I had seen him before. Then I remembered a performance I went to at one of the local colleges, a performance I wanted to see. I had forgotten this because at the time my arm was in a sling because of a fall on the ice outside my parent's house and I probably wasn't focusing properly on things happening around me. Once he finished talking with the architect and his crew was unloading equipment, we started talking. David told me that he had gone through a divorce since we last met and was living alone and traveling to New York City, freelancing various projects--mostly making kitchens since he was a cabinet maker. I listened carefully as he talked, focusing on his intense blue eyes that sparkled in the intimate auditorium as we shared different parts of our lives. We spoke until we both had to get back to work. He was so nice to talk to, and being an artist himself, he spoke of sculpture and his background constructing theater sets. I understood why he was now constructing the new stage and lighting grid. It was fascinating to just "bond" with someone out of my usual circle Our chats were wonderful as we gained insight into one another. After a few days of talking, he extended an invitation for me to come and visit him at his house and have dinner but it was several months before I took him up on his offer. One time I did try to go, but I accidentally left my parking brake on while driving and ended up burning the brake lining, affecting two of the tires. Embarrassed, I called him from a pay phone since cell phones were not in wide use, explaining the debacle. It took me a while to regain my courage to try again. Things between us revolved around having fun and getting to know one another better. Our talks were enlightening as we went on several "informal" dates, had dinner, and on some level there was always depth that brought us closer. He was so easy to talk to and a fresh person in my life. The age difference of fifteen years was never a factor in our relationship because we just got along so well. At the time he was forty and I was in my late twenties. There was an obvious mutual attraction between us but also a looming caution in my mind.

I finally went over for dinner and was startled at the austere environment he lived in. There were naked light bulbs awaiting fixtures, a combination wood and gas stove, two faucets for hot and cold water, old furniture, and a furnace that sounded like an erupting volcano. Obviously he had been a bachelor for a while and did not have much in the way of comforts, like a warm house. The house had been restored back to its original form, keeping the old drafty windows and stucco work intact. His house was always clean, the windows sparkled and his mother's handmade curtains were a nice touch, but it always looked like a cleaning frenzy had taken place before I came over. Overall though, his home lacked a "cozy" feeling. I took note, but since my main residence wasn't with him, there was not much I could do.

He came to the Church every day with the "guys" as they tore the stage apart and slowly built a lighting grid that would give the performances an artistic flair. I always saw the crew when they first came in and at the end of the day when they left. It was hard for me to focus on my job as I sat at my desk upstairs either entering new membership information in the organization's database or counting money from the last performance. I would have much rather been downstairs talking to David. The auditorium was certainly in shambles, but they say things have to get worse before better. The construction activities went on for almost a month, and then one day David was crouching under the stage and needed some help with clamping a board underneath the structure. Since I happened to be walking by, I obliged and crawled underneath with him. The moment was certainly interesting as we both pretended that was normal as we lay there looking at each other, but it was anything but that. I did not mind being useful, but secretly wished I could just throw my arms around him.

Intimacy was on my mind and probably his as well, but I wondered whether I knew him well enough just yet. My feelings still surrounding my immediate family and my condition were unresolved and reared their ugly head every so often. I just loved going to David's house on the weekends and since David was a wonderful cook, we cooked and talked. Sometimes we took long walks into the woods as he spoke of future plans to clear forest and make small parks. We strolled and talked about world events, spirituality and the land. We would walk in a way that I can only dream of today. Finally one day we embraced as if to end what we both had been feeling for so long. It was so still and quiet except for the rushing waters below the hill we had just climbed. I completely let myself go at that point-- we were just two people who finally found each other. I didn't even care that I had MS. The waters of the shifting creek below us flowed in such a powerful way, changing direction rapidly, like my own life until that point. As we walked back with the sun setting behind us, I knew I had to go back to my parent's home. Reality showed itself as I started to make noises about leaving. He cooked a quick dinner, pasta and mushrooms with garlic and butter, one which reminds me of that day even now. He tried his best to get me to stay. After dinner I left. Intimacy felt comfortable soon after our new discovery of each other

I revealed my disability to him quite early in the relationship. Multiple sclerosis was not something he knew much about but, interestingly, his grandfather lived with it and died in his fifties when David was less than a year old, in the 1950's, when so little was known about MS. The revelation about his grandfather was not told to me when we first met since MS was never something that mattered much.

Later on in our relationship it was revealed to me that David had fathered a child at 19 when he was in college, a daughter he had never met but who sought out her birth father and mother. His daughter is now in our lives and adds a new and richer dimension to David, the father. Apparently he had searched for her over the years but his daughter at age 35 decided and was successful in unsealing the adoption records. Once she did this, regular visits now make up for the lost years. Sometimes David makes trips to California on his own to see his daughter, quality time that the two of them need to spend together.

Once while visiting David, a snowstorm made it impossible for me to get back to Delhi. My father was on the other end of the phone when I was forced to reveal my whereabouts that included an overnight stay somewhere other than my bedroom in Delhi. "Where are you? It's pretty bad outside," my father said, concerned. I wasn't sure how to handle the situation, but chose to be honest in my answer without revealing my actual whereabouts. "I am near Worcester, you know, going towards Albany?" "Oh, but that's so far, are you with David?" His question told me, and possibly my father, that on some level as a father, he needed to let go.

David is a master carpenter with myriad skills. His sensitivity towards people is obvious, particularly when he deals with older clients, people who have difficulty reaching high areas or bending over to open low drawers. To them he makes practical suggestions that help to make their life easier. He is mild mannered and does not like conflict. Our relationship began slowly and we even dated other people but continued to talk on the phone for hours and always made a point of getting together when he was in town. When we first met, my MS was not the entity that it became and never got in the way of my walking, hiking, biking or pursuing anything active. I did tire then, but as soon as my physicality started changing I struggled with how to voice my concerns. The year was 1992 when I began to show subtle signs of something being wrong. I continued to work at the arts center and David continued to live upstate and make trips to New York City. I lived in my parent's house once Mom, Jai and I moved back, and my father came to stay when he wasn't busy traveling.

I finally got my own phone so David and I could chat whenever we wanted to. I would come to his house and blare music out of my parked car window as he built an addition onto his shop. He talks about my "young" ways back then and said it always helped break the monotony of his everyday life. Occasionally he would bring some friends home from the New York City, some who did not speak English and some who had been friends of his for years. I was not always comfortable in these situations, particularly when I stayed over and did my best to communicate. I managed but always felt so much younger than everyone else.

During this time, I decided to break off our relationship, not because of David but because I felt there was something else waiting for me. This "something" else was more of a feeling than anything. I clearly remember that day as I sat at the breakfast table with him after one of the snowstorms, eating a wonderful meal and finally informing him that it was time for me to "move on" for a while. I started visiting my good college friend in Rhode Island, five hours away. I was young and had a car so I would drive out on the weekends, eager to meet a handsome Indian boy she was going to set me up with. I ended up in a long-distance relationship with someone who was not my type. My new relationship was handsome and charming, but I soon realized how much I missed David. Needless to say, all this was very tiring, particularly the long trips to Rhode Island.

Spending time apart did not stop David from continuing to support me in every way possible; he was always in my life. He was dating a woman with a young son, a doomed relationship, sort of like the one I was in. We just lived our separate lives, although we did talk on the phone occasionally, just not as much as before. It was as though we wanted to be together, but apparently (as years later he told me) I wanted to test my wings and be free until I was ready to settle. He may have been right, because I needed to do something with my life, following my instincts to begin a career, meet other people or just be involved in something that interested me. I had known David for about a year at that point and life kept moving on as it seems to, but despite the changes, David was never far away.

My life focus changed in 1994 when I began a new and first-ever injectable therapy for MS. The demand for this medication was so high that people who wanted to try it had to enter a national lottery and wait their turn. I waited an entire year before my number came up. This was a very disruptive time in my life as I dealt with horrible side effects of a treatment that I thought would take care of my condition. Life seemed particularly difficult as I dealt with side effects such as flu like symptoms, malaise, fever that lasted for at least three months until my body gave into this assault. Despite these problems, there was never a thought in my mind of not trying the new medication. I had stopped going to Rhode Island but continued to work at the arts center for another year. David and I were in touch with each other as I entered a world of confusion with my new therapy.

NEW THERAPY

. . . .

A shot every other night during the week was an inconvenience I could handle, since this was the first therapy for this condition besides the conventional steroid and some chemotherapy infusion-type medications. Looking back, I was blinded by the very common feeling of hopefully finding the answer to the problem. The first night I gave myself the much awaited shot, it felt as though someone had hit me over the head with a blunt object, creating a splitting headache and shakes one gets with a high fever. Shots became a part of my life, and it was common for me to give myself injections during concerts in my last year at the arts center. One time when a concert was underway, I looked around and seized the opportunity to give myself a shot in the vestibule where the ticket table was. A lost audience member walked in and stared at me as I whispered my way to explaining that there was nothing illegal in my actions. That is a funny memory, one which makes me chuckle but also makes me sad if I think too much about it; there I was, giving myself a painful shot, not knowing what it was really doing.

I left the arts organization in 1995 and attended classes that I thought would amount to going back for my Master's in counseling psychology. I became fluent in understanding people, perhaps because my own difficulties had had a sort of humbling effect on my personality. I thought I would use this new-found nature of wanting to listen to others' plights to my advantage. In other words, listening to others might put my own trials in perspective. From the very beginning I leaned towards not wanting to make my situation so terrible that I could not function. I used my savings to take classes at a neighboring college. My thought process at the time was to be a professional in an area such as counseling since that was something I had sought but never resorted to, or maybe being in a position of authority would allow everything in my life to fall into place. My money was used to take about two semesters' worth of credits without a long-term plan. As I was pursuing my classes, my anxiety level and blood pressure had begun to rise steadily; my life consisted of trying to pursue the status quo without my realizing I needed to take extra care in things that were no longer second nature. Many activities, such as rushing around all day or doing several activities or errands at once, were not happening without falling, making mistakes and just getting tired. Years later my blood pressure continued to rise incrementally because of the new therapy, which added to the already escalating stressful life situation. The three months of horrible side effects just made life unbearable. I continued to work and study in spite of this.

David continued to support me in my efforts and sometimes came to the campus to pick me up after class. We would go back and stay at his house and discuss all the new theoretical knowledge I was acquiring. His participation in my life was sincere and I didn't ever feel alone.

The constant toxic effects of the medication were awful, but somehow I continued on with this therapy for ten years. As I have found out in retrospect, all that was unnecessary because at the time the fear involved in not doing toxic medication was a far worse calamity than the illness itself. The medication gave me peace of mind but became harder to administer as the years went on. Sometimes in the evenings my father would give me a "thigh" shot because he seemed to have a steadier hand than I did in those days. The novelty had worn off, and my mother was having to deal with all sorts of insurance bureaucracy because I was on her insurance at the time. Skipping a shot occasionally wasn't bad, and I did that more than once since my body was so sore. There were no relapses or set-backs except some very slow degeneration during my time on this therapy; however, my blood pressure continued to slowly rise. I did feel myself to be mentally a little "off," something I couldn't articulate, but physically I was managing. I could tell that David was not pleased with watching me go through this therapy, but he kept his opinions to himself.

The plan to pursue something else was now nagging me--my full potential was not being tapped, and I just knew in my heart that something better was around the corner. The "corner" at that point could have been anywhere. Life was waiting for me to make my next move. Shortly after I finished my counseling classes, a bookstore owner approached me with an offer to work at a new bookstore in town for minimum wage. He was the husband of the owner of the store, someone who had been an acquaintance for many years, another person with MS. The thought of working at a job, any job, was appealing, even if the pay wasn't much. So I agreed. The store, on the Main Street in Delhi, was lovely; it was also a very short distance from my parent's house, a distance which I walked in high heels more than once in any given day. The very thought of doing that now seems completely foreign.

The bookstore owner's husband was very awkward with his condition because he had the MS "swagger," an unbalanced way of walking with the legs spread widely apart to maintain balance. This way of walking is known as "ataxia." I felt for him, never thinking I might follow suit. I shuddered every time he walked across the street to get coffee, navigating his path across Main Street back to the bookstore. It was so obvious that something was terribly wrong with him, in his case neuropathy, where the foot has little if any sensation and of course this leads to fatigue. The "lassitude" type fatigue, or a tired feeling beyond just feeling worn out, which envelops someone with MS is a daunting experience.

At that point, the decade mark into my disability proved to have been an important milestone. The year was 1997. Eleven years of having MS. I knew I was walking a little "funky" but probably still able to seem better than the bookstore owner's husband. Multi-tasking and fatigue did not seem to inhibit my activities much at the store at that point, or at least that is what I thought. A bizarre experience alerted me to a new happening one morning. I was very used to talking to customers, answering the phone and ringing up sales items simultaneously, until on that morning the phone rang while a customer in the store asked me a question. "Mona, are you alright?" My expression was one of complete confusion and annoyance. I could not stand the fact that the phone was interrupting my thought process! I responded, "I'm alright, let me just answer this annoying phone." Normally this would have not been a big deal, but "executive" functioning is often a cognitive or "thinking" issue affecting many people with MS. But I didn't know that. I just could not shift my attention calmly. People tell me all the time that phones annoy them too, however this was not always the case with me, particularly when a job demanded it. What makes this experience different from someone just having a bad day is the fact that it was just uncharacteristic behavior for me. My sound threshold for some reason seemed lower. I couldn't stand any confusion. Fortunately, this lasted only for a couple of weeks (until it showed up again much later). So now I had to pay attention to the cognitive side of my condition in addition to the physical changes.

A local attorney came into the bookstore one day when she'd found out I would be leaving there after the closing of the bookstore that year. She asked if I would be interested in working in her office; I spent the next five and a half years working with her. The attorney's office was enlightening. She was interesting, educated and a great attorney. In my time there, I played various roles, including "sweet receptionist," where I was always willing and able to provide the client with my best possible attitude, "guard dog" when I protected the attorney from angry clients by providing a buffer between her and them, and "cultural conversationalist" which was my ability to share my life and cultural experiences with others. So, I was always pre-occupied.

I started looking for ways to expand my horizons beyond the small-town existence that had been my life for the past ten years or so. The urge to be brave and pursue much larger things propelled me. Going to medical school at first seemed outrageous, but what did I have to lose? I loved the human body, health and all the ways to be well. I was always interested in healthful eating and physical activity. I discovered the field of occupational therapy (OT) through my readings and internet searches. Finally I was satisfied I had found my new vocation. This satisfied all my cravings to learn something completely different, something that might actually amount to a career helping others. I could just see myself with a client in need of someone else to put their problems in perspective so that they could figure out what to do. Essentially that is the main tenet of OT, helping others to help themselves, since human "occupation" is a great motivator. In this case occupation could mean being a mother or a stock broker. How interesting all this was! MS had become an occupation of mine through which I would help myself and others. Occupational therapy, a very misunderstood profession, was something I badly wanted to understand and be a part of. Once again, this pre-occupation with helping others was another way for me to cry out to help myself; I just didn't know how. First I thought my career might be in counseling, but now OT!

A new symptom, "foot drop," was slowly beginning to express itself. Foot drop is a very frustrating symptom because the nerve that helps raise the front toes to clear the ground when walking gets progressively weaker, causing one to drag the foot. It began with my walking on the outsides of my feet because the soles of my shoes were showing an uneven slant. Soon it was clear that my left leg was showing a weakness that my right was not, and my ankle would twist on uneven surfaces because it had no strength. The falling began very slowly; I often blamed embarrassing incidents on carelessness. At that point my own belief was that being "clutzy" or a stone appearing out of nowhere caused falling, not the MS, because I was too coordinated a person to just "fall."

The new MS symptoms that were obvious in the bookstore owner's husband, were now happening to me. It made me all the more determined to use personal experience to make a career. Clinicians study these symptoms and even research them, but do they live them? This new energy was exhilarating and yet oxymoronic, because physically my energy was not abundant--but what a great direction all this was leading to! My partially visible "handicap" now gave me a handle to portray myself differently, by way of my life.

GRADUATE SCHOOL – THE NEED TO SUCCEED

· ·

I was thirty-six years old and working at the attorney's office. Every day I awoke pleased that I had a new direction, and every day seemed to have purpose. I started taking morning walks with Felix, my thirteen-year-old dachshund, who was not terribly pleased to walk at six in the morning but who put up with my insistence that he accompany me. I used that time to plot my strategies and dream of becoming an occupational therapist (or OT, as they're known). I felt strong. I told people that I was going back to graduate school.

I searched the internet for schools with good OT programs. Several schools showed up in my searches, but the one I chose to pursue was Washington University School of Medicine in St. Louis, Missouri. This particular school attracted me because one of the faculty members had done research focused on MS and occupational therapy--how impressive this seemed! As I dug deeper, I realized that the path I had chosen was not going to be easy. At the graduate level, most institutions required students to have taken an entire year's worth of pre-requisite classes: anatomy and physiology, statistics, and some fundamental science courses.

A few of my classes from Wells could be used to fulfill some of the program requirements at Washington University. For the rest, I enrolled in some classes at the local college in Delhi; others I took online, including statistics. Fortunately, it was not difficult to negotiate online academics, but the subject matter was difficult. My obsession to make something of myself, using my diagnosis as a measure of strength, made this year of pre-requisite coursework easier than I had thought it would be. I stayed on at the attorney's office so that I could pay the tuition for all these classes. That is how determined I was. With the classes completed before I had even applied to graduate school, I felt a real sense of accomplishment. I achieved the 3.0 grade point average required by Washington University and then moved on to the required observation time with a working OT. For this part of the requirement, I made arrangements with three different establishments--a hospital and two schools for developmentally disabled students. The OT for the school system was young, energetic, independent, beautiful, and so powerful with her students. She walked quite rapidly down the school corridors, tossing her blonde hair from side to side while talking to me. Fortunately, at that time I could keep up the walking pace, just wanting to be her!

During this time, I lived in Delhi with my mother. Jai had moved to New York City and my father was working in Michigan, staying with his brother. Mom and I did well living together, but my father's decision to live in Michigan created tension between my parents. I continued giving myself shots every other day, without my father there to help.

One day during my anatomy class at the local college, the professor interrupted class to tell us that airplanes had just hit the World Trade Center towers in New York City. It was September 11, 2001, a day none of us will ever forget. I worried for Jai since he was living near the site of the catastrophe, but thankfully he was fine.

As I continued with my pre-requisite work, the time seemed right for David and me to visit St. Louis and the school I had chosen. Once I found St. Louis on the map, my determination to get there was the only thing I could think about. David and I battled two snowstorms to get to the Midwest, putting in late-night calls to the airlines in case of cancellation, all in order to visit the campus, to take a preliminary look and meet some faculty. The department had determined that I was on the right path with my coursework and that some of the undergraduate classes I hoped would transfer did so successfully. It all went very well. St. Louisians were friendly and down to earth, and I was ready to apply to the school and take advantage of everything it had to offer. I spent the summer writing essays, filling out the application, and learning as much as I could about St. Louis and OT. When David and I finally headed there in the spring, the weather was a little muggy--I had read that the climate was extremely hot and muggy in the summer, but somehow it didn't seem like a worry at the time. Getting settled into the school was more important to me at that point than how the hot, humid weather would affect my MS.

I never thought about not being accepted to this school. Given that it was the only place I applied to, maybe I should have worried a little. I knew that Boston College and Washington University were competitive in OT, but never took into consideration that Washington University's occupational therapy program was ranked #1 nationally at the time I applied. Why should any of this have mattered? I could just feel my destiny calling and I pressed on.

One morning while I was working at the attorney's office, I walked to the post office to gather the office mail. While I was there, I decided to check our family post office box as well. Among the envelopes was one addressed to me from Washington University. My heart started thumping and I felt faint. I opened the envelope and read only the first line before breathing again. I had been accepted, was now a part of the new class in Washington University's OT program, and would begin my coursework in the fall. Oh, did I feel important! Things were in place now. All my determination had got me this far; now for the rest. I had no idea what to expect.

I had itemized the cost of getting to St. Louis and wondered how I was going to come up with the money. Before I left, I held a small party to say farewell to friends, and some of them had collected some money for me. I was touched by their kindness, but the amount would not be nearly enough to cover the trip. I appealed to the wealthy father of a friend who, much to my surprise, sent me a check sufficient to cover the remaining cost. Now I knew I was on my way. I said goodbye to my mother and also to my father, who had returned to Delhi. The hardest person to leave at that point was Felix, the companion who had listened to my mutterings and plans over all those months. I cried for hours. I was determined to keep my eye on the new circumstances, though.

David and I loaded his van and headed off to the Midwest. We stopped and saw friends along the way and made a real vacation out of it. We stopped at Niagara Falls and did the boat tour. I noticed that my left ankle was weaker than the right. I took a fall on the grass before the boat tour, but somehow I paid it little attention because I was focused on my new path. Finally, after many stops and many miles, we reached the Gateway city to the Midwest, with its famous Gateway Arch that has come to symbolize St. Louis. Everything felt different to me now. I looked at the medical dormitory and what was to be my life for the next two years. It was warmer there and the sky seemed huge. I don't remember ever seeing "big sky" like that in the Northeast.

The occupational therapy department at Wash U, which was what everyone called the school, had set up a number of orientation activities, and I attended them all. The distractions were so many that saying goodbye to David was not as difficult as I thought it would be.

Things were going along fine. I set up my room, met people in the program, and finally attended an introduction of faculty in the OT auditorium given by the president of our program. This auditorium, where our main lectures would take place, became home to a hundred students that year. As I listened to the president's speech and looked at our new faculty, I felt proud to have a place in that auditorium. "You are the best and have been chosen to attend Washington University's program in OT. Welcome to St. Louis." Everyone in the class was young, smart, enthusiastic, and ready to begin.

For the next two years, every day of academics was grueling. Two students dropped out because they were not able to keep up. The rest of us attended long seminars, wrote innumerable papers, and went off campus to various facilities to accomplish related coursework. I attended class all day and returned to my room ready for a nighttime of work. My frozen salmon in my little freezer was ready to pop in the upstairs microwave. A small salad would round off my evening meal, necessary sustenance for a night of studying. Fortunately, staying organized is one of my strengths, and that helped keep things flowing smoothly enough that I could keep up with the lack of time to do anything but study.

By my second year, the stress and heat started to affect me both physically and cognitively. When I went home for vacation, I traveled through many different airports (at the time, that was possible for me since my mobility was not really affected to the point where it was hard). I was still managing my walking and fatigue. It was such a relief to get away from the grueling academics. Just to sit down in one of the terminals at a Starbucks seemed like such a treat! After one of my trips back east, David and I drove my car back to St. Louis so that traveling in the city could become a lot easier for me. St. Louis is a well-marked town, so I had little difficulty finding things, and during my first year there the streets had started to grow more familiar.

I was particularly happy to have my car, because walking in the heat had become more difficult; I had definitely noticed more tripping and falling. I kept quiet about these things, mainly because I wanted to be like my classmates. I chose to accommodate these developing problems by not walking as much or by spending more time out of the heat in the air conditioning. I fell a few times during the "fitting-in process" with everyone else in my environment. One day, I was walking back from class to my dorm along the tracks of the metro (the city's little subway system), and I fell hard enough to cause a bus driver with a bus full of people to stop to ask if I was OK. That was a turning point. I made an appointment with a physical therapist to see about getting an ankle foot orthosis (AFO), something we had just learned about in one of my classes. The AFO is used for persons with neurological conditions such as MS when they have symptoms of foot drop. In this condition, a damaged nerve prevents the foot from lifting, causing the person to drag the affected foot along the ground. Trips and falls are inevitable!

The physical therapy program was right across the hall from the occupational therapy program, so the clinic I went to for evaluation was in the same building in which I spent my day. The evaluation entailed a great deal of walking up and down a therapy room to determine the proper bracing for my situation. The hot

St. Louis sun was trying its best to enter the therapy room, which was air conditioned and had long blinds in front of the windows to keep in the cool. After the evaluation, I was sent to a facility that makes the braces, and within a week I had an instrument that completely changed my walking. I could now keep pace with classmates more confidently without worrying about the big cracks in the pavement that could cause falls.

Weather was still a big issue, though, because it just fatigued me to the point where I had to sit in an air-conditioned room to regain my strength. In that humidity, I was having difficulty managing a short walk outside or even sitting in a shaded area. I approached my professors about testing accommodations; specifically, more time and a separate room for testing. They readily obliged. This helped me enormously, because distractions such as page turning, coughing, or shifting around in seats made me completely lose my concentration and ability to think. Such situations reminded me of the bookstore incident with the phone. Something similar happened to me while we were being tested on body parts in the cadaver lab, bodies that we had dissected as teams. I found it impossible to stand in long lines with my classmates while we identified different anatomical parts before the timer went off and the line went on. One tall female student with an all-knowing sort of attitude was always in front of me in line, and her presence was a guaranteed distraction in that high-pressure environment. My mind just could not process the information quickly enough. Setting up accommodations was a good move because it became obvious to my professor that time constraints stressed me out horribly.

Not for a minute did I regret my decision to come to St. Louis, though there were challenges I hadn't figured on. Sometimes I just couldn't avoid hot parking lots or shopping at hot times of the day, given my schedule. I tried to buy groceries and run needed errands on the weekends to avoid getting into those hot situations. Things finally got to the point where I appealed to the MS Society in St. Louis to borrow a scooter from their loan closet to use for going back and forth from class to the dorm. Even with the AFO, walking was becoming harder, combined with the added stress of academics and heat. So far, I had devised a way to walk more easily, had testing accommodations in place, had my car to avoid travel difficulties, and now had use of a scooter to get around to class and some nearby shopping establishments. Heat, humidity and MS are not compatible partners, it was clear.

When David and I had first visited St. Louis, I remember that we walked quite a distance together without my needing an AFO. Obviously, things had changed since then, and I was starting to resent my situation. The brace was large, which meant I couldn't wear just any shoe--it had to be a size larger than normal. My female classmates, mostly from the Midwest, were in their twenties and gorgeous, and there were only two males in my class (OT seemed to be a predominantly a female profession).

On the other hand, everyone--students and faculty as well as our dorm maids--was nice, and we all had camaraderie. After all, we were enduring a tough program together, complaining to the housing staff all the while. I didn't have any family nearby except for David's brother and his family, two hours north of St. Louis. I had made contact with the MS Society, though, an important step for me in more ways than one. I became acquainted with someone at the MS Society who later became a friend. She was on the other end of the phone when I called about the scooter, as well as a time before that when the heat was so hard to deal with. She proved to be a compassionate listener. As it turned out, she was a graduate of my program at Wash U., and because she sounded very nice I had trouble keeping composure and holding back the few tears that were trying to escape. Eventually, we met for lunch, and she gave me hope as well as some anatomy books, having been through the ordeal of the same graduate program. Although she never advised me, she had a comforting nature, and that was what I needed. She has since become a friend, even visited me in upstate New York, and although we don't talk frequently, our exchanges when they happen are very meaningful.

During my second year, the program became more difficult. The courses now demanded more application of what we had learned, which involved more activities outside the classroom, which of course meant more mobility issues for me.

Thinking back, I realize that I worked hard at just maintaining a normal demeanor. A walk to the medical library, even though it was through an air-conditioned building, sapped my energy. I remember being elated at the fact that I had walked that distance. All this had to be accomplished before I even began studying! It just felt good to be like other people. Though part of me realized that there was no chance of being like everyone else--even though the possibility of being "normal" was slim--it certainly helped me get through some situations that I could not have negotiated had this insistence on being normal not been my way of thinking. I walked to my car every morning in the parking lot wearing a heavy backpack, just like any number of other students. I sat in classes and long seminars all day only to go back to my dorm, cook dinner, and begin my evening shift of work for the next day. It took more effort than if I hadn't been dealing with MS--it was exhausting in fact--but I never missed a deadline or a class in two years.

My classmates and I did have fun together in my two years at Wash U. We found creative ways of studying some difficult material, including anatomy and social theory. Some of us would frequent coffee shops, libraries, or friends' houses to study. We drew colorful pictures of bones on index cards and tested one another. One evening, a few of us decided to have dinner, study, and watch a movie at a friend's house across the park from where I lived in the medical dormitory. It would have been hard for me to walk across the park, so a friend kindly dropped me off in her car. Needless to say, after a long evening of drinking and eating without much studying, we all woke up and realized that there was no way to get me back to campus since no one had a car and my other two friends had biked their way over. Plus, we were all nursing the proverbial hangover. One friend decided to put me on her bike and have me pedal while she held on to it. My hand-to-eye coordination and balance were both quite poor, and I was troubled by a great deal of weakness, so the plan didn't work because I kept falling. Then, much to my own surprise, I discovered that if I did not look up at all the stimuli around me and just looked at the bike path, I didn't fall. This strategy became a topic of conversation in one of my classes the next day. Someone pointed out that horses wear blinders that shield the sides of their eyes so that they can concentrate on the task at hand. Thanks to moments like these, I continued to learn and take in all sorts of new information.

One day, an MS specialist from the local hospital came to our class as a guest speaker. When she asked if anyone in the class knew someone with MS, my entire class raised their hands! The speaker was stunned until she realized I was the one they all knew.

Our rigorous academics continued as we endured lack of sleep, stress, continuous testing, and oral presentations. I had been taking out student loans to fund my education, pay dorm fees, and have some money to live on. I wasn't worried about the mounting costs, since I planned on obtaining gainful employment to pay back the loans. But even though we all walked for graduation in May of 2004, it wouldn't be over until six months of fieldwork was completed after the academics, sort of like a residency.

As the time for our graduation drew near, a female classmate approached me and said, "Would you like to be our graduation speaker?" Nothing came out of my mouth until she finally said, "Well, will you?" I was very flattered and agreed to do it. That whole time period passed in warp speed as we finished classes and tied up loose ends.

Suddenly the big day arrived. David and my parents came to see me graduate. Our robes were magnificent in the Washington University colors, black and green, with "don" style hats. We graduated in the Elliot Chapel on the main campus, a building with beautiful stained glass, along with students graduating from a variety of programs. I was not the only class speaker that day; there were several others from different programs. We lined up outside the Chapel along with our faculty and the director of our program. The orchestra started playing, and the atmosphere was completely overpowering. The moment must have absorbed my whole being because, although I could see the stage that I would soon be standing on, it didn't seem to affect me much. But I do remember finding it hard to stand for a long time. People in the audience stood as we marched in, led by our faculty and then the class valedictorian. I sat down next to the other speakers, two from the doctoral OT program, the guest speaker, my co-speaker, and other faculty, on a raised stage with the orchestra and audience in the level below us. By now I must have been a little worried because I don't recall any of the speeches except the introduction that led to my standing up and hearing words such as "impact" and "multiple sclerosis." The tears started filling my eyes when our director started speaking, so by the time I stood up, I was pretty much a mess. I got up to the microphone and couldn't compose myself enough to speak. The only sound I could hear was that made by my tears falling onto my paper—a sound made louder by the microphone. It was, in fact, the loudest sound I had ever heard. I couldn't look at my classmates; I was too embarrassed. I just hoped time would pass and I would somehow start speaking. Finally the emotion passed and I was able to begin. My speech was short. I remember seeing David in the back of the chapel with his camera. I remember my classmates looking at me. At the end of my time I hung my head and sat down, mortified. When I finally looked up it was to see a standing ovation. The entire audience was on their feet with arms extended towards me and clapping vigorously.

In a way, all this was a dream come true for me. I had made it through what I had set out to do. Now photographers took our class pictures individually as we exited. A faculty member hugged me and said, "Mona, this is just the beginning." I assumed she meant the beginning of my "life," but she probably meant that I still had six months of clinical fieldwork to complete before I received my degree. All the events that followed showed me that more was ahead than I realized.

The year was now 2004. David and I moved into his house together after I finished my courses. Then my clinical work began. I have never been through a more exhausting process in my entire life.

My first fieldwork site was at the National MS Society office in St. Louis. I had to travel back to St. Louis to do this fieldwork. My clinical instructor was Suzanne, the OT and graduate from my program who had been employed with the society for several years--the same woman at the other end of the Society's helpline to whom I first spoke when I arrived in St. Louis. She structured a fieldwork proposal that my department accepted and, since she was an occupational therapist, working at that site became a reality for me. On days when fatigue consumed my soul around afternoon time, it was not unusual for me to lie on the floor of the office as employees stepped over me; I was simply the new fieldwork student with MS. The feeling was one of belonging, just like an airplane that returns to its hub city after its daily round of flights. I worked hard and met deadlines as expected, as Suzanne and I made sure that assignments were acceptable to the high standards demanded by my school. Once those three months were completed, half of my clinical work was over.

The second site that I attempted was about a five-mile drive from the campus every day for another three months. The setting was very different from the MS Society. There was no air conditioning in the building except for the "office" upstairs, and that was not where I spent my time. There was a long flight of stairs, maybe about twenty steps, that I ambulated up and down, sometimes several times a day. The stress, heat, and basic ambulation wore me out to the point that there was very little energy left to focus on my actual fieldwork. At one point the fieldwork director had to be brought in to assess the situation, since my performance was less than acceptable. She sat down as my fieldwork instructor began a predictable line of questioning, things you would normally ask any other student under the circumstances. The problem was that this set of circumstances was anything but normal. I burst out in tears. I simply had no strength to articulate what was really going on: fatigue, St. Louis heat, and stress from trying to pass my clinical, as well as trying to cope with physical and emotional changes that no one seemed to understand, not even the great profession of occupational therapy. I felt pathetic and lonely. How could I stop crying long enough to make any sense? My fieldwork instructor was one of the more understanding people, but pressure on her was enormous because, after all, she was running a shelter for men who were addicts, many of whom were mentally challenged and trying to pull their lives together. Here I was in a situation where I was unable to get through half the day without feeling a total loss of control. Once my performance was being questioned, it made me even more nervous. I had no ability to tell my body to behave differently; it just couldn't.

The toughest part of the fieldwork occurred once a week during the big "shopping" caper. We all went to the farmer's market in a small van with a broken air conditioner so that the men in the shelter could go around with money I gave them to buy items to be cooked the next day. The idea was nothing but noble for the men, since this was part of life skills training. The issue at hand was that I couldn't function--and I was supposedly in charge of this undertaking. The heat prevented me from counting money to give the men because I lacked hand coordination and was missing synapses in my brain. I couldn't tell a five-dollar bill from a ten once I was overheated. Basic ambulation around the outdoor space seemed impossible, but I forced myself to do it. Once we returned, I had to climb down the flight of stairs that I could hardly see at that point because of my blurred vision. I was so deep in a bad situation that, like a person who has gone insane, I tried to do the same thing over and over, expecting different results. Needless to say, I did not pass this fieldwork.

A similar problem occurred at another demanding fieldwork site where there was too much ambulation and stress: once again I did not know what to ask for. These issues overshadowed my real purpose, which was passing fieldwork and generating confidence in my instructors. Unlike the previous two settings, the instructor here was immature, younger than me, and not at all like the caring ones in St. Louis. I doubted she had the capacity to even begin to understand my predicament, which dashed any hope of getting through successfully. I had no energy left to prove to her that I was as qualified as my cohorts.

One of the OT faculty members, who meant nothing more than to help me, sat me down and asked me a battery of questions.

These questions seemed absurd to me, since they all revolved around how much I could walk in a given day. She insisted on specific measurements; i.e., how many feet or meters before I got fatigued. She was only trying to gauge my limits in order to put some accommodations in place. But MS does not allow for absolutes and is famous for unpredictability. My energy varied from hour to hour, and under stress I had no idea how I would perform. Before I began my clinical in a new setting, I had to return to St. Louis to complete a "remediation" program that was protocol for students who had difficulty getting through their clinical. This meant I had to arrange for a room and incur more dorm fees and travel expenses just to go through remediation. One time while in St. Louis, I fell ill during the remediation and left a voice mail message on an instructor's office telephone, only to have her express her disdain that I had missed a session because I had left the message on a voice mail that she never checked.

Things were becoming so difficult that I was losing all hope. I just couldn't handle the environmental barriers and the normal workload. Once I finally completed remediation by writing more papers and play-acting more clinical scenarios with my instructor, I flew back to New York to begin work in a setting with developmentally disabled students. All this caused me to lose time trying to pass the necessary fieldwork. I started visualizing my diploma and began to wonder if I'd ever obtain it.

My feet were pulled out of the fire by a compassionate therapist who saw what was happening and how much I did have to offer. In the beginning she did not seem too sure of how to make fieldwork possible, but then she said, "we're OT's--we should be able to figure it out." Her response instilled in me a sense of camaraderie that no one else had expressed. She made it possible for me to excel by creating an environment where my physical limitations were made more "neutral." This meant a reduced caseload spread over a longer time, using my scooter to get around, and giving me more responsibility under reasonable circumstances to see how well I did. For example, I went to the kindergarten of one of the schools by myself, without my instructor, to meet with clients to do therapy individually. She made me eternally grateful. In hindsight we both wondered if Americans with Disability Act (ADA) standards were as easy to put into practice for everyone. After all, it is up to the person to ascertain their predicament and make requests. My personality was such that it was a tall order for me to make my wishes known if I believed that I would be creating tension and difficulties for others, in this case my instructors. Accommodations were offered to me, but my thinking was that they were unnecessary and it would be best to do without them if I wanted to be like everyone else. I realize now how silly that thinking was. All this was a tough lesson I had to learn over the years since then. It has taken a long time to create "my normal" as the status quo, as opposed to trying to achieve what everyone else calls their "normal," something I probably couldn't accomplish anyway.

The fieldworks should have taken six months to complete but ended up taking me three years, given the remediation work between disasters. I was no longer in school but out in the clinic, having to prove not only to myself but to others that I could do this work. There was no way to be just another fieldwork student. I had too many challenges facing me. What Washington University and I both did not comprehend was that no amount of remediation was going to help because my spirit was breaking. At the end of this last fieldwork, much to the school's surprise, I not only finished, I excelled. This fieldwork felt different to me, like I was actually connecting not only with my clients but with my coursework as well. Washington University was so pleased with my clinical instructor in my last fieldwork that they flew her out to St. Louis to attend the big American Occupational Therapy conference as their guest. They awarded me my diploma in 2007 after all academic requirements were successfully completed.

Starting at this point, my mind could make no decisions, my morale was the lowest it had ever been, and I lost all sight of what I had set out to do in the first place. I had systematically endured failure, did not feel competent, and had wasted a great deal of money traveling between upstate New York and St. Louis. What absolutely blows my mind is that my MS at this point was still in a better state than it is now. I had endured enough stress for a lifetime, affecting my condition more than I ever knew. I know it now. Now I am disabled, living day to day in a way that accommodates the MS, picking and choosing activities that I am able to do. But it is interesting to reflect on how I proceeded after Wash U. and the fieldworks were over.

MY "NORMAL"

L ater on a psychotherapist who I had seen to sort out all these feelings after these traumatic fieldworks told me that under pressure I became a "performer". This is how I survived stress. By performing the way I thought people wanted me to, I would make everything turn out fine. I would make up the energy later by taking a nap, so I thought. I knew I was having some difficulties, but I never thought it might mean an end to my dreams. Once all the fieldwork and academics were over, I was living with David and trying to get used to making my new residence "my house." There was a great deal of adjustment involved as I tried to live my life after Washington University. I had always planned on having a career after finishing graduate school. In order to accomplish this next step, plans were made to sit for the board exam that would give me the ultimate designation "OTR"-- occupational therapist. That way, I could work privately or in a setting that would allow for a career.

In order to sit for this exam I was entitled to some accommodations by law. I had a vague idea of what to ask for but soon learned that sometimes accommodations were not specific to my situation. Just because something meets the Americans with Disabilities Act standards doesn't mean the accommodation will always work for you, as I soon found out. Had there been fair clinical instructors out there as in my last fieldwork, my efforts might have been more successful. My fieldwork instructor and I had understood together that giving me more time to complete a task did not always result in a good outcome because once I became fatigued I could not add 2+3. Current ADA standards are meant to help a large number of persons with various disabilities, but what if you don't fit set guidelines? The first time I sat for my occupational therapist licensing exam, accommodations had to be in place in order for me to have a fair shot at this lengthy exam. I asked for things that seemed pertinent such as a paper pencil test, extra time and a separate room. The paper and pencil test would eliminate staring at a computer for five or six hours, which would have exacerbated the visual difficulty (my vision has been compromised ever since the optic neuritis attack in 1986). The separate room would free me from distraction (since "higher level" executive function is compromised by the MS) and the extra time would allow for rest breaks. The National Board which certifies occupational therapists (NBCOT) readily granted me all those requests. It took me three attempts to try and pass the examination. After the second try I realized how taking the exam in two parts was probably the only way I could have passed. A computer test would have been fine; there would have been less time involved than with a paper and pencil test. The reason for this was cognitive fatigue--quite simply, the brain got tired sooner and my thinking was affected. Also, holding the pencil for long periods caused my hand to fatigue. I once read a study that illustrated how normal functioning students improved as testing went on whereas persons with cognitive disability deteriorated as testing went on. The separate room was fine except that it only had a fan, was stuffy and became hot during testing, which caused further fatigue due to MS-related heat intolerance. NBCOT refused to give me the test in two separate parts and told me to stay overnight in a hotel to lessen travel time, as if that was the problem! I can only assume the reason for not granting me the test in two parts is the possibility of cheating. So, the accommodations gave me little help toward meeting my "normal" since I did not fit the guidelines. It is probably immaterial that I did not pass, since using the license for employment has become much less of a possibility than it seemed when I entered graduate school with such high hopes. I was tired of fighting at this point. I now had a master's degree in a professional field but no license. I continued to learn a lot about the disease process and my functioning within it.

It wasn't until 2005 that a medical episode changed my life. Things just were not feeling "right" on a particular day. David was talking to me in the kitchen and said, "Your t-shirt is going up and down" as my heart was visibly pounding through my chest wall. The mirror in the bathroom showed a reflection of someone I did not recognize. She looked positively sick. My eyes were noticeably bloodshot. Interestingly, during all this time no one commented on the eyes that were protruding in their sockets. When I spoke there was a thumping that I could always hear, one that came from my own chest, it was my heart! When I climbed the stairs in our house, all twelve of them, my heart thumped extra loudly and my clothing over my chest bounced up and down as if it were alive, causing me to sit down once I reached the twelfth step. The gasping for air was the nail that sealed the coffin, which it may well have done, literally, had I not gone to my doctor friend for what was a previously scheduled routine visit. A hypertensive episode with blood pressure of 220/180 landed me in the emergency room. After much deliberation and process of elimination, the doctors decided that the culprit may have been the Betaseron, the interferon medication which had been in my system for over ten years. The shock of this episode was not so much that this had happened but the reaction of the medical community; no one took responsibility for what happened, particularly not the pharmaceutical company that manufactures this product. My mother had had to engage in insurance wars with the company just to get me the medication in the first place, now this. It is my impression that others have gone through hypertensive episodes similar to mine, but unfortunately our say is drowned out in the overarching medical mill. "Stop all your medicines, including vitamins," were the words of the attending ER doctor, who proceeded to order painful potassium infusions by IV to increase that particularly important nutrient that had reached very low levels. Clearly no one knew what to do and no one understood what was happening. It took three long years after that episode to plant my feet firmly on the ground once again. Meanwhile, recovering from this shock wave was no small matter. I did not need this aggravation, plus I was withstanding all the woes of not being able to find suitable employment--or any employment. My father, who passed away on June 9, 2009, had been giving me some money to manage every month, but all this ended in 2008. Every month was a struggle, but somehow the bills got paid. It was during this time that I met with a clinical psychologist who used neuro-psychological testing questions to get an idea of how my brain functioned at that point. This testing continued for a number of days to prevent fatiguing during testing. She gave me activities that tested my ability to multi-task, use reasoning, logic and visual ability (like picking similar things out of a mass of objects) to get an idea of how my brain functioned. The results of the test became clear as I discussed them with her. My verbal ability was relatively untouched, but manipulating language in analogy-type questions or using my vision to match similar objects all suffered. My ability to process information quickly was not the same as before my diagnosis or as that of someone without MS. The way things were explained to me by my neurologist was that there is an information highway, in this case the corpus callosum connecting both brain hemispheres, which had incurred damage. The corpus callosum is a heavily myelinated structure (which means it is covered by a fatty substance called myelin) which is being de-myelinated and in the process slows down the traffic going across it. In the MS process, the myelin is in jeopardy because it is the target of immune system attacks. So, thoughts or new information were taking longer to travel, therefore I took longer to comprehend some concepts. I was told that this was not reflective of my intelligence, just that I had some challenges. This was overwhelming news, but at least my verbal ability was unimpaired. So if I took a test such that requiring multi-tasking or fast thinking as in standardized tests like the SAT's or GRE's for graduate school, my results would be poor, and they had been. However, if given essays to write in lieu of multiple choice tests, I did much better. Cognitively my brain had been affected by MS and overall brain demyelination, where certain aptitudes were intact and others were not. Stress and fatigue most definitely affected certain functions such as concentration, multi-tasking, ability to deal with interruptions, and mental stamina, all of which just made working a normal job very difficult. Employers have limited patience and tolerance for this compromised behavior, even though persons with disabilities are protected by the ADA. Now I had to figure out how to live comfortably or just how to live.

Since moving in with David not only gave me the freedom to be myself, there was no reason to move back to my parent's house. Besides, once I returned from graduate school in St. Louis, we both assumed that moving in together was a logical next step. I worked extensively with vocational counselors from New York State, trying to find some employment. By chance a connection was made at the local State University of New York in the Student

Disability Center. There were no benefits with this job, but at this point it did not matter. Something was definitely better than nothing. On a hot day in the summer of 2007 I went up to the college to speak with someone about the position. Once I figured out where to go and got my car finally into a parking place, I got out with my cane to begin the long walk across the hot blacktop. Once I began this journey across the parking lot, I soon realized that the heat was unbearable. I barely made it in the door, only to find steps that led upstairs. Quickly I spotted an empty chair and quietly sat down. Once I gathered myself and my thoughts, I asked the janitor if there was an elevator. Now all I had to do was gracefully go upstairs and speak with the director of student disability services.

The director, younger than I, sat in a large air-conditioned office with a very clean desk, which made me wonder if he did any work. I could hear myself slurring my words since heat and walking fatigued me; while answering questions he asked me. Somehow, things worked out and I got the position.

My first week was hell. The department was in the process of hiring a secretary, furniture was being moved around, folders were moved from one desk to another just as I was learning the ropes of this new job. The process to someone with cognitive disability was like telling someone without sight to read the mail on the table. I was beside myself in an unfamiliar room, made distraught by ringing phones, student traffic and conversation, new computers and a slate that I did not even know how to begin to write on. Everything I have read about cognitive dysfunction, multi-tasking, concentration, distractions were all right in this room. The director kept saying how sorry he was that things were a mess, but he didn't have a clue how that mess was magnified in my cognitively compromised world! To most people MS represents a loss of physicality but there can as much loss in the brain and in performing simple actions that normally one would take for granted. It is this "missing of beats" that makes employers frustrated--but not nearly as frustrated as the person experiencing this sensation that what once was is no longer the case. These days I hear of Iraqi war veterans who have returned home with traumatic brain injury, going through cognitive issues similar to this.

After the first week some dust settled, but that was the longest three months I had spent anywhere. Students with different forms of challenges, learning disabilities, physical challenges, emotional challenges and the like came to this office, which had an adjoining room, for testing. Sometimes I would read the tests to them, or put tests on the computer so they could test separately in a quiet room. I had made lists of duties, had a wonderful rapport with most students and came in every day to do my job. Then the mistakes started happening. I started missing important information told to me by the associate director, particularly on how to handle information involved with the tests. One day as the mistakes were mounting and I started getting nervous, the tension in that small office was obvious. I even started bringing in my scooter so that walking wouldn't wear me out but that turned out to be such an inconvenience, an eyesore and always in the way. When the phone rang, my heart stopped because for the life of me I could not transfer calls properly. I hung up on people, disconnected them, and even transferred them incorrectly. One day a student came in and I handed him his test. On the outside of the manila envelope there was a note written by the professor that specified that this student was not to leave the testing area until a certain time since his classmates had not taken the test yet. Some students had told their classmates about test questions if they had already taken the test. Someone in the room asked me a question just as I handed the student the test and I completely missed the important note on the envelope. Once the student completed his test I let him leave. The associate director was livid once she found out what happened. The work environment was a snake pit for me. I just could not handle anything that required responsibility of an important kind and distractions or chaos could not happen if I was to do my job, but we all know that in the real world that is not possible. The director called me in and relieved me of my job. To this day I don't think he fully understood what was happening, even though he was the person in charge of others like me.

Resigned to the fact that working a "real" job was out of the question, I next decided to set myself up in such a way that something could be accomplished, even if it was something of my own. Structure was something I craved ever since the Montessori school days, preferably something created by me at my own pace. Now more than ever this has become a way of life for me, out of necessity. Many things have happened since the MS therapy was stopped, graduate school was over and my father passed away. Financially there was no help, since employability was less and less of a reality; at least David would be carrying the household expenses whether or not I was here. Social Security Disability was something I thought I should apply for even though all I heard from others with MS were horror stories. I made an appointment at the local Social Security office, and the procedure to fill out paperwork was underway. A stern but cordial woman took down all my information in the utmost professional way possible without any concern or comment as to my current predicament. I suddenly realized that many, if not all, of the people there, seated in similar cubicles, were in similar situations to mine. My initial reaction was to feel helpless--this was a long shot. Once the information given was adequate, I went home and was told to expect paperwork soon. Filling out the questionnaires was a difficult process. My procrastination necessitated a phone call to the name on one of the forms to let them know I was working on the questions and would meet the deadline, which I did in the nick of time. Fatigue and malaise made putting one foot in front of the other difficult.

One afternoon I received a phone call from the Social Security office. First I thought it was a tele-marketer with her low, hard to understand voice. Much to my surprise, the government had accepted my disability application. When I found out, I went outside and walked up and down, flailing my arms with happiness. This was not charity but money owed to me by the government based on my small earnings. This meant I could pay bills without agonizing over things every month. My monthly income was now based on what I had put into the system so far, which was not much given my age and lack of work experience. Monthly checks are deposited into my account to this day, even as I look back on that melancholy day when I sat in the drab office with the stern woman, not thinking I stood a chance. The amount is very little in the current economy, but with careful orchestration the monthly bills get paid. Paperwork for disability discharge regarding my federal student loans has also been submitted, and after being conditionally accepted, to my knowledge the loans have been permanently discharged. Now I needed to develop a decent dialogue with the private student loan people. The best way, interestingly enough, to maintain good relations is constant dialogue with them to keep them up to date on my situation. They have been apprised of my situation and all sorts of medical documentation has been submitted to explain the fact that something went terribly wrong after graduate school, something that was not part of the plan. The private student loan industry is a business, regardless of how much they project a human face; they're interested in the return of their money! Since David is the cosigner and responsible for 40% of the total, amounting to several thousands of dollars, this is a constant worry for me. A number of people manage to "work" the system, but there is a contingent of us who have ended up on an un-chosen path.

A recent exacerbation at the end of March 2008 brought my existence to a halt, because within a day I could not walk. In all my readings on the subject of MS there was talk of this possibility, but never did I imagine it happening to me. Why now, I thought, at a point when things were going well? Upset and emotionally disheveled as I was, the internet was the only way I knew that could provide me a way to find an answer, support or maybe even a lead to something. With tears streaming down my face, I doubted any immediate relief to my predicament. The search yielded a puzzling answer, one that in all my years of searching never popped up before. Something called Low Dose Naltrexone had provided countless people with MS relief within twenty-four hours; the science behind it made complete sense. The mastermind behind this medication is a Harvard neuroscientist by the name of Dr. Bernard Bihari. If it had been a charlatan from some unknown establishment, I might have continued on with my search. Dr. Bihari was challenging the established MS protocol, particularly by proposing that the immune system in persons with MS is not overactive but underactive. This goes against the very thinking that has been ingrained in every MS researcher's mind, until now anyway. Dr. Bihari has now passed on and at the time had retired from Beth Israel Medical Center in New York, but he'd had a general practice in internal medicine in New York City for years. His research into autoimmune conditions including AIDS and Crohn's led him to find beneficial effects in MS as well. Voraciously, I read anything to be found on the subject of Low Dose Naltrexone (LDN). A neat package of information was exciting news to be shared with my neurologist, who would naturally have some questions given that no clinical trials, only medical hypothesis, had established the efficacy of this medication for use in MS. The reason for lack of clinical trials was that Naltrexone had already been FDA approved for something else, namely, opiate addictions; in those cases, LDN was used at a much higher dosage. The patent on this medication had run out, and there was no money to be made by the profit-hungry pharmaceutical industry in doing research. Why would anyone pay millions to study an already approved medication? So profit was dictating the blockage in allowing this medication to enter mainstream thinking in the minds of most people's MS doctors. I had collected all relevant data and scheduled a visit to my neurologist. At the previous visit, when results of the MRI had been discussed following the nasty episode in March, it was my choice whether to engage in traditional MS therapy which left only one choice, an everyday injection to modulate the immune system. Because of what happened in 2005 with the last interferon shot, I wasn't going to consider any of the interferons; besides, my thinking was now beginning to change. But this time I had ample information to discuss another, "different" oral medication with my neurologist, Low Dose Naltrexone.

I did generate a dialogue with my neurologist, but it did not go as well as I was expecting. I felt at a disadvantage because I wasn't feeling strong when I went to see him. I was having an exacerbation at the time and was having difficulty walking, so I was using my scooter, mainly because I was so tired. The neurologist did not see eye to eye with me on the workings or "efficacy" of this medication. I even used the only plea I had in my arsenal at that point, "Doctor, look at me--what have I got to lose?"

PART III

CLARITY AND INSIGHT

"A bird doesn't sing because it has an answer,
it sings because it has a song."
--Maya Angelou

LOW DOSE NALTREXONE, MY ONLY MS MEDICATION

. . . .

At this point in my narrative, I'm describing my present life. How strange to suddenly be writing in the present tense most of the time!

Well, that neurologist and I were never going to agree, so I went home and approached a friend who is a doctor. She gave me a script, and my current neurologist (yes, I found a different one) regularly gives me this medication.

I have been taking low dose naltrexone (LDN) every night before I go to bed, starting in 2008 when I had that awful exacerbation. Traditional neurologists are beginning to prescribe this to people, given the overwhelming anecdotal evidence of its working for people's benefit. Our medical culture relies heavily on scientific protocols, and I do think that is important--but so is quality of life! It seems like every other day there is news about some pharmaceutical company getting sued for not being honest about side effects of this or that medication. How are we supposed to trust anyone these days? This extends to the food in our stores and medication that is advertised on television and magazines. Anyway, I would call the so called effects of low dose naltrexone a placebo effect, except that in my case the positive effects have lasted beyond five years. It is by no means a wonder pill in the sense that it does not help with my walking or heat sensitivity but it has helped with the fatigue. I know it has. If I understand the workings of LDN, it may not be having a direct effect on my fatigue but rather an indirect one. It has raised my endorphin levels so that I have a sense of well-being, and maybe this is giving me a better outlook in general. This is something else I would recommend to anyone with MS. Why not try it? It has no side effects except for some minor sleep disturbance when you first start it. Personally, I have chosen LDN and some lifestyle changes to tackle a very complicated condition and situation.

I say "complicated" because it is not just the condition itself, it is the people and dynamics surrounding the mystery that is MS. This unending journey from one end to the other has been a lifetime's worth of work for me. In order to keep things moving and flowing, I try to keep my focus on the important things and priorities that make living easier. Low dose Naltrexone is an interesting part of this picture because it works silently in the background. I have listened to several people with MS tell me their stories about obtaining this medication from their physicians. The bureaucratic institutions that I mentioned earlier include certain doctors who for some reason dislike out-of-the-box thinking even if it may do their patient some good. By no means should one embark on a solo voyage searching for answers. See what the MS population is saying about LDN. Beware of websites and individuals who spew nonsense, good or bad. Stay with reputable sources, as I did when I did my research. As I have found out, this medication is used for other conditions as well.

EATING FOR MS

. . . .

N ow, this is a tough area to explain and one of the most important. Let's think for a moment how important food is in our lives. When I am in the supermarket and watch people around me as I continue to learn about health, it makes me sad to see the number of processed foods that go into people's carts, or the sugar-laden sodas and other fast foods. Now if I take a bite of anything processed or "wrong" for my diet, I can taste it! The other evening I had part of a piece of pie made with Crisco and could not get rid of the horrible sticky feeling on the roof of my mouth. When I bake, I use oil, never butter or lard. I am more focused on some of our garden herbs like lemon balm, chives and lovage that would complement our meals made at home. I think it is important to eat with the seasons. Everyone talks about diet, the proper way to eat, what to do, what not to do etc. We all have to be so careful with our health.

In the process, I became interested in the Roy Swank diet for MS and really enjoyed reading his explanations of what current research is unveiling in the circulation area. I really wish he were still alive, because I would find a way to meet him. He made discoveries as a doctor back in the 1940's, when he was seeing an increase in MS and similar conditions. He implicates fat as being hard on the circulatory system and systematically explains the rationale behind this theory. Apparently over the years he had treated many persons with MS through diet alone, with great success. Not everyone he treated could stick to the diet, and those who didn't were disabled much sooner than those who did. Following his reasoning, I concentrated my efforts on watching what worked and what didn't. As per Roy Swank, I gave up eating saturated fat. My old way of eating changed, specifically eliminating all processed foods and fats, and about two years later, I felt the changes. I also avoid all dairy. Even the occasional feta cheese in a wrap is not fine--and no cow's milk products whatsoever. According to Dr. Swank, the fat in milk is the culprit, but I have discovered an allergy to the milk protein itself. I don't even miss the cheese or ice cream. The tradeoff is worth the sacrifice. Dr. Swank wrote a book explaining his philosophy, and his nurse compiled a number of wonderful, tasty recipes, a book which is a permanent fixture on my kitchen shelf. Back in Dr. Swank's day, sugar was all right to consume in large amounts. So, using common sense, one has to make the appropriate changes in light of more recent studies by reducing sugar in the recipes laid out in the book. I adhere to the Roy Swank diet with a few modifications which included no dairy, not even skimmed milk. (He does permit no-fat milk.) I have been on this diet for five years and am happy to report that not only do I feel well, I maintain my weight and look healthy.

(An Italian vascular surgeon whose wife has MS recently made the discovery that persons with MS often have compromised venous systems. This is what Roy Swank had been talking about in the forties!)

My own research and reading has enabled me to move ahead very successfully. The diet portion of this picture is an important one; lifestyle is equally important. I often look to professionals for answers I am unable to obtain. But lifestyle change I've done all on my own, and anyone can do it. Adding to the confusion are the fad diets out there that become media fodder. If Oprah Winfrey is doing a particular diet and the public is interested in her situation, they will follow her example, or if Montel Williams is losing weight and looking good and turning his MS around, the public will follow that. It is only normal for people to want to help themselves. I realized this, but I also found it all so intense and expensive to do myself. A few years ago, for some unknown reason, I developed asthma. It has taken me several years to learn not to over-analyze why this was happening, particularly since my health and make-up are so complex.

I keep track of books on the market that talk about diet and MS. There are others with MS who have discovered the diet connection and want to help persons challenged with MS. There is another theory out there known as the metabolic theory. Embracing dietary modifications and changes to one's way of eating is not just following a set of rules, it is a way of life. It has become that for me anyway. The small milestones of success are not drastic in the scheme of things, but when it is two in the afternoon and I am not overcome with MS-related fatigue, I realize how far I have come.

Our supermarket does a nice job of stocking fruits and vegetables that go with the season. For example, the berries are now out, not like in the winter, and other good fruits include pears and certain apples. Our pear tree has blossoms and it should be a successful season. The dandelion, which is the bane of most gardeners' lawns, is most potent in vitamin A. One can witness birds and chickens eating the dandelion flowers and then the white fluffy ball that comes afterwards. In the early spring the ramps, a member of the onion family, make a delicious meal with a touch of vinegar. In this way I watch what comes out of the ground and look to that for guidance in my own eating.

These are not huge discoveries, just small ones that make a huge difference for me! Something is making me feel good, and I think one of the things that accounts for it is the way I embrace my philosophy of food based on all my observations and readings on the nutrition that is best for me. I just keep thinking that so much of my supermarket is in my back yard with the burdock root and dandelions and chives which make a nice vegetable entre or just a nice garnish. Last night after a long day, dinner consisted of nice Italian tuna fish, mixed into lemon balm, chive flowers, red pepper, capers and onion with a touch of balsamic vinegar over some egg noodles. I said what I always seem to say when something tastes so satisfying, "I could eat this every night!"

Certain MS diets are strict on gluten, sugar, corn and many other items. I have a simple belief that what works for one person might not for another. Those things should be eaten in moderation, like most things. If I react badly to something I do not attempt to eat it. I drink wine in moderation.

So, my conclusion with the whole diet debacle has been to watch suspect foods which cause bad reactions. I eat with the seasons and off our land as much as I can. If I want something to satiate my sweet tooth, I use Dr. Swank's suggestions for baking (using less sugar) and eating a low- to no-fat diet. I never buy anything off the supermarket shelves with any unpronounceable ingredient or anything that is obviously processed. I buy organic poultry, vegetables, fruits, eggs and fresh fish. We also have our garden in the summer time.

I maintain this simple regimen and seem to be keeping my health in balance. As things have turned out, I consider diet one of my main treatments for my MS.

MOBILITY: "WALKAIDE" STYLE

· ·

B ack when I was in graduate school, my walking began to deteriorate. I was aware of how difficult things were getting, particularly walking on uneven surfaces and over sidewalk cracks. To someone with a normal foot, these things hardly matter and are not even thought about. My foot was becoming compromised but I could not keep up with the pace of deterioration. I started tripping and falling, sometimes without any visible obstacle in front of me. So, as things went on, and the process of "losing" my foot (not being able to signal the brain for movement), I developed foot drop, also known as "drop foot." Deterioration continued as I started dragging my foot along the side of my body because it was acting "dead," refusing to move or lift at the ankle. The left foot did not move willingly, my knee didn't bend and the leg didn't lift. What a challenge it became to do normal activities!

I used the AFO that I got in St. Louis for about six and a half years, throughout the remainder of my education and fieldworks. Slowly my circulation started getting worse. My leg started atrophying since it was always in the AFO, never working to walk in any way. Also, I was getting tired of having to wear a particular kind of laced shoe always a size larger than normal. The functional foot had to wear a larger shoe at all times since shoe stores do not let you buy two different-sized shoes. All this was turning out to be no fun at all.

The time was right for me to search for an alternative. I knew there had to be a different way to walk. Well, I found something that I have been wearing for a while since I made a changeover. I found the WalkAide, which is a neurostimulation device that straps on under my knee and taps the nerves to lift the ankle, giving me the movement in my foot to take a step. I like to think of it as "animating" my ankle. There are a few important points worth discussing about this device. And they are: cost, positive effects and negative effects. I'll be objective about the WalkAide even though I have had a real love/hate relationship over the time I've had it, which is close to five years now.

I made the acquaintance of a person in a local shop when I filled out a form online to express interest in the WalkAide. No sooner had I finished filling out the form, my phone rang. Technology can be spooky at times, but since I had supplied my phone number on the online form, it's not surprising that someone called me. I made an appointment and went to the office to find out more information. A technician evaluated me and used a device that looked like a tuning fork to see if he could elicit a nerve response in my leg. This was explained to me as looking to see if one branch of the peroneal nerve in my leg would elicit a response to lift my toes. I understood what he was doing because of my knowledge of anatomy. There are two branches of this nerve, one in the central nervous system which was non- responsive due to the MS, and one in the peripheral nervous system which was unaffected by the MS and might respond. Well, the nerve did elicit a response and my toes actually moved, after not moving for years. So, I was a candidate for the WalkAide.

The next step was to go to another facility where a WalkAide trained orthotist walked up and down a hallway with me in order to program the WalkAide to work with my particular stride. Once that was accomplished after many hours, I was sent home with the device for two weeks to start using it and get used to not being in a brace. I did this, and some re-programming had to be done in order to tweak some movements. During the two weeks, I had a few accidents and fell because I was putting too much faith in the device, but since then I have learned how to properly use it. The next step was to somehow figure out how to pay the almost $5,000 that it cost.

I appealed to the MS Society and worked with an individual who got me $1,000 from the Chapter and then helped me fill out forms to appeal to some charities. I got a little more money but certainly not enough to pay for the device. My best friend from Wells College came to my rescue—she said she knew that I was meant to have this device--and she made up the rest of the money. So now I never use a brace.

The positive effects of having the WalkAide involve leg and foot activity. Using this device requires a great deal of energy, since a non-responsive foot is being made to "work out." Gentle stimuli are sent to the peroneal nerve, bypassing the brain, tapping the nerve which in turn lifts the toes and moves the ankle. I do not have to wear shoes that are too big, I can wear sandals—not to mention dresses--without a brace, and I can even walk bare foot securely. I have decided not to use the brace, just to walk more carefully and slowly with just the WalkAide. The whole idea behind the device is to get my foot out of a brace and walk as normally as I can.

There are two electrodes in the device that go over the nerve. I ask the MS Society to help pay for a year's supply of electrodes when I start running out. It is important to not shave the leg with a razor that might irritate the skin under the electrodes. I did this and one slightly bloody spot where I had cut my skin affected the entire area. I managed to contain the damage, but not without the huge inconvenience of not being able to wear the WalkAide for long periods to allow for healing where I had shaved my leg. Now I wear it when I go out but keep it off when I am inside the house. This way you also save the AA battery which runs the device. A second precaution is the understanding that this device is not the complete answer to your walking issues. When I first put it on, I thought I could take off walking fast--and nothing was further from the truth. Often times I forgot to "wait" for the stimulus to engage with my stride and moved too quickly; the result was numerous falls. But like with most things in life, I got used to it and now I value my little cuff, keep it safely in a plastic bag at night, change my electrodes every two weeks like I am instructed to, change the battery and walk slowly, not expecting a miracle.

MY MS SUPPORT GROUP

• •

When I was young in India, I was all consumed with wanting an "identity." Now, at fifty, I feel like I have one--or rather, one was assigned to me. Now I don't care about ethnicity, am well settled, and live with a disability which puts me in a different category altogether.

When I was struggling with wanting to create a new life for myself in Washington D.C., I wished I had searched for someone to talk to about my MS. At the time I was afraid to do that. But when nothing was going as planned, I certainly could have used a support group. Even though the neurologist who first diagnosed me told me that a support group is just a bunch of babies whining about MS.

Then I met a great group of people.

In the nineties I was ready to talk to someone about my journey so far. It was a beautiful summer day as I recall, the setting was a quaint-looking hospital in the Catskill Mountains in Delhi, New York. I was concerned about walking through the doors to look for the room where this meeting was to take place. But I was more concerned as to who I would find there. This event was advertised in a small-town paper, so who knew what to expect? Local people with MS, that's all I could assume. I found the room and walked in. It was not a large group, and clearly I was the youngest person there. Exchanges included one's name, number of years diagnosed, occupation, etc. Everyone was pleasant, the group even included a doctor with MS. During that meeting I felt as though the foundation had been laid and I was not alone in my battle for understanding.

That particular group waxed and waned over the years, losing members, gaining new members, changing locations and always looking for hope. Today two of the "original" members, including myself, continue to try and assimilate new members, disseminate much new information and above all, welcome anyone who wants to talk about MS. There always seems to be a new person who comes to the meetings, not a surprising event given the rising numbers of those diagnosed.

One of our founding members, Jean, who always came to the first group, is now in her sixties but continues to be an important influence in my life. She has had to go to a nursing home because life just became too difficult to manage without assistance. Also, she lost her home in a terrible flood. At the beginning of my journey, Jean and I continued our friendship through difficult times. She continued to drive until she could not anymore. I remember how she had gotten her steering wheel adapted with a knob for easier turning. Early on I remember how that adaptation influenced my wanting to learn more about ways people with disabilities could make their lives easier, which became one of the reasons I went to occupational therapy school. Not only that, but Jean drove me to her brother's house in a different state so I could sit for an exam to enter graduate school. If that isn't caring and friendship I don't know what is.

Today, Jean remains active in the politics of her nursing home. She is a friend to many, a grandmother and also, despite difficulty with her hands, an avid painter. I will always remember our special friendship, lunches out and mutual personal battle against

MS. Today Jean no longer meets with our group but has started a group of her own in the nursing home.

Our new support group meets in another small town, Oneonta. We have moved locations several times but we now have a secure location; we meet in a church building once a month. The atmosphere is safe and inviting. Our group does not have strict rules (not that we ever did). It's a very casual, laid back group. We advertise our meetings in the local paper and I send out monthly email reminders to the group. New members bring new energy and wisdom and help our mission of being there for others.

People come to the group as their needs dictate. My co-facilitator, Phil (someone who has come since the inception of the group), and I believe that all people who have joined our ranks have different needs, and we try to provide them with compassion and understanding. We laugh and cry with our group because, after all, no one willingly signed up for a lifetime of challenges. We all see the importance of working through our feelings in a safe and healthy way. I personally think that all of us battling chronic illness deserve at least that much.

OCCUPATIONAL THERAPY
FOR MY LIFE

. . . .

I spent two years in graduate school and another three to complete my clinical work in order to get my master's degree in occupational therapy. So the scales were already tipping more on the wrong end. The additional three years happened because I couldn't keep up in clinical environments because of my MS, as well as a whole lot of anxiety. I was always fatigued, with the accompanying cognitive problems. I have spent years wondering if it was a wasted effort getting my degree but not subsequent employment or a license. Many thousands of dollars in student loans later, all I had to show was a diploma in the standard red case. As I continued to wonder and question my hard work over those years, a good friend of mine simply asked me one day if I could imagine life without that education. All the wondering came to a screeching halt as I responded, "No". All those hours I spent in anatomy and physiology class and the cadaver lab, and countless hours spent writing papers and more papers, gives me a more clear understanding of not only my schooling but a lot of hard work. That is only part of the picture. Accommodations that I make for myself every day, like knowing how to properly exit the bathtub with one paralyzed foot (more specifically peroneal nerve palsy secondary to MS) or how to put on clothes despite poor balance, how to deal with fatigue while prioritizing the importance of daily activities, reading medical literature--and the list goes on. Aside from these "tools" that my education has provided me with, the importance of human occupation has made my life so rich that I do not miss not having "real" employment. Human occupation is not a theory or model like it was taught in graduate school, it is a way of life. Quite simply, occupational therapy is what humans do every day that makes life meaningful to them. I try to write every morning, part of a routine I am trying to develop. Today it is raining and reminds me of my childhood and monsoons in India as well as the years in Jakarta. All the more meaning for my day! My occupations include being David's partner, my gardening, maintaining my home, and writing, involvement with my MS support group, doing my own research on health issues, being a sister and daughter, and so on. These activities in some way dictate my every day function. My time is my own now, and I use every moment of every day to find that meaning that gives human occupation importance.

I always think of occupational therapy as helping others to help themselves. But before I could help myself, I had to get out of my own way. Sometimes one has to let go of certain situations in order to succeed.

One neat trick David came up with was tying a rope to my laundry basket which enables me to lower my basket full of clothes down a flight of stairs without having to walk down with the basket in my hands. Walking downstairs with anything in my hands has become impossible since I now need both hands, one to hold the railing and the other for balance. When my laundry is done and I have to come back upstairs, I use the step by step method, putting the basket up a step and climbing up behind it. I also take a cup of coffee up the stairs to my study by placing the cup a step or two ahead of me, following it up the stairs. This may take a while but at least it is safe. This way there is no coordination of movements that I have lost.

I really don't have to go to the gym to work out; I am too busy trying to figure out the various ways to make my life easier. There are always solutions, I just have to find them.

The bathroom is definitely a major fall risk for someone with limited mobility. Everything is hard with the foot drop. Adding spasticity to that means a stiff leg that neither bends nor moves. So, I did not go through an occupational therapy evaluation and get a series of grab bars in the shower or around the bathroom. I worked with an occupational therapist friend who visited me once. There were things I could do, it turned out, in order to get in and out of the tub. I felt that too many grab bars might throw me off and instead of helping, would make matters worse. After demonstrating what I needed and how I planned to accomplish my moves, we settled on one vertical bar on the wall next to the tub that I grab with my left hand, entering the tub with my functional leg, pivoting slightly in the tub, grabbing the bar then with my right hand, and pulling the affected leg with my left hand into the tub. Exiting the tub is doing this process in reverse. The affected leg exits first, followed by the functional leg while holding onto the bar with my right hand. The point here is that every person's needs are different. Someone else in my situation may choose a different method.

The main thing I always come across is the feeling of being overwhelmed with most things facing me in a given day. This could be a "routine" activity such as driving to the store, taking a shower, calling the doctor's office, or completing errands that have been nagging me. I have found it very helpful to make lists and then break down tasks.

Regarding shopping, small lists are more desirable than long ones. Besides managing small amounts of groceries, the whole experience is less fatiguing. In the summer time it makes much more sense to go early when the weather is cooler. In the winter I just monitor the snow forecasts carefully. If I have another errand, I sometimes do just that one without combining too many things all at once. I know that all things do get done. It is important not to get exhausted doing them. For anything that requires walking, I am thinking of experimenting with two canes to help provide support to my left side. If it is too hot, I use my little mobility scooter so that there is no issue with too much standing and walking. Using aids should become second nature the more you use them. I feel it is my right to have almost the same experience as anyone else when going out and about. I know it has never been the same as everyone else for years, but I can try my best to make it at least enjoyable!

MY ROAD TRIP TO EMANCIPATION: OFF TO NORTH CAROLINA!

. . . .

So, I have spent most of my life figuring out how to make things easier and a way to enjoy my life. I had worked through so much agony and confusion but knew in my heart I had been living with acceptance and needed to experience life. I was finally put to the test. A Facebook friend and I were chatting on social media one day when I complemented her food choices and presentation. She is a registered dietitian and I am a cautious consumer with extensive knowledge of MS diets. So I made an innocent comment during that exchange, "Wish I could be in your kitchen!" and this comment was then the focus of a small class reunion! My friend lives in North Carolina, and she proceeded to invite a number of us to her home as well as to her family's lake house. I gulped when I realized what had taken place. Was I up to this challenge? Fortunately, one of our other friends offered to drive down from Vermont and pick me up—and I decided I could do this, after all.

North Carolina is very hot and humid. Could I do this? I had many months to decide how to proceed, as well as watching a whole lot of excitement build around this whole event. I had been working on the life rehearsal for this event in my mind for a long time. In my mind, there were days when it seemed like a ridiculous proposition. But these friends were the beloved Wells College women I had spent the best years of my life with! I had a ride down with one of them, someone I wanted to get to know better, so what was holding me back? Finally we got closer. I procrastinated packing my suitcase. Then I felt overwhelmed and packed the bag in my mind and left the actual packing till the last minute. Obviously, nothing seemed real until my friend came to my house to pick me up!

I ended up zipping the bag up the evening she arrived and was to spend the night. Everything seemed too easy as I gathered toiletries, which somehow seemed harder to do when I'd go to my mother's house forty-five minutes away.

David and Heather sat down the night before and finalized the route. A calm feeling swept over me because I wasn't the one driving and neither did I have the responsibility of making the route. That would have been stressful for me. Just packing the darn suitcase was enough. So we all had dinner and made it an early night. I was really enjoying my friend Heather's visit to my house and not really thinking about the next day and the long trip.

The next morning came and we had a nice breakfast before taking our showers. We loaded Heather's car (which thankfully had lots of room to fit our luggage) as well as a set of crutches and a brand new euro-style rollator that another friend Mary bought me for the trip. My new rollator is collapsible, which helped. We were ready to go! We started out, made several rest stops and chatted all the way down to Lynchburg, Virginia, where we stopped for dinner and an overnight stay in a Best Western. Our destination was Apex, North Carolina, which was about four hours from where we were in Virginia. One of the advantages of the rollator was being able to put bags on the seat to relieve poor Heather. We soon realized that there was a biker convention staying at the hotel. It was quite sweet actually, as people black and white bonded with their group. We were lucky to get a room but had never thought to mention my disability to avail of some accessibility. It would not have mattered, because the hotel did not seem ADA compliant; it was without elevators, sliding doors (on the contrary, it had very heavy doors) or enough handicapped bars in the bathroom. Interestingly, none of that bothered me as much as it did Heather. She could see my struggles. I managed just fine, but the woman at the front desk was sympathetic enough to carry our bags up a flight of ten stairs plus a walk to the room. She must have been aware of my struggle, or else she knew the hotel was breaking the law or that we just looked exhausted. Anyway, the room was adequate and we got a good night's sleep and a complimentary breakfast the next morning. I was just going with the flow, something I didn't think possible in the rigid life I carve out for myself at home.

We started out the next morning with the occasional rest and fuel stops. Once we got to Raleigh/Durham, North Carolina, we started stressing out because the directions got muddled up and Heather was screaming at her GPS which (according to her) was being uncooperative. After calling our friends, getting directions and getting lost a few times, we finally made it. A few of us had gathered at the Apex house; some had not seen each other in many years. Sweet reunion! Some had not seen me or my disability since the Wells years. It was a powerful moment, but quickly none of that mattered. I've thought about that and realized that the MS is now just in my movements without a real personality change. I felt like we were all at Wells, just that I didn't move in the same way. I was still me, thank god.

My friend Sheri's house was beautiful and she made us all so comfortable. I stayed in a bedroom that had been made handicapped accessible for her mother in-law who had disability because of a stroke. So, here I was in the best possible situation I could ever hope for. The house had central air conditioning, easily maneuverable space and a handicapped room with attached handicapped bath and shower. The heat in Apex was humid heat, my nemesis. But I was well protected.

The fun I had with my friends was like magic and a rare treat. We went on a few adventures, and I was included in ways that made everything possible and enjoyable. One day we visited a pottery studio, a place where one of us knew of the artist. My friend Heather is a potter and wanted to meet this artist. We stopped for lunch along the way--tough to do with the heat we faced getting from the car to the building, but it wasn't a problem. We finally got to the studio, but the way into the building was not possible for me, mainly because of the ninety degree day. I could have managed the steps, but the heat made it impossible for me until we were allowed in through a side door on one level; along with the artist's assistance, it enabled me to be a part of the whole experience. I was humbled by everyone's help and good nature. That was a long but fulfilling day for all of us. Wow! I could actually use my rollator to sit in situations that demanded it, fold up the device and put it in the car as needed. Everything, including me, was working like clockwork.

My friends even got me into the swimming pool which I swore I would not get into. The ability to bend my knees and enjoy movement without gravity pulling my joints or the reduction of debilitating spasticity was very refreshing. I would stand straight by the poolside then fall back as they caught me and gently lowered me to the ground, and eventually I "scooted" to the pool where someone else would make sure I made it into the water. I will say that I was so humbled by everyone's good nature and support that the MS seemed irrelevant compared to everything else going on.

We had another memorable adventure, a three-mile hike on the tobacco trail. I was included in this without much thinking! I sat in the rollator with yoga straps around both feet to prevent them from dragging, an ice bag to help with the heat, a hat and sunglasses. There were five of us who went, plus me. Four took turns pushing me three miles along a sometimes bumpy trail with fascinating foliage along the way. There were other runners, bikers and walkers who were also using the trail. Thinking on this, what a sight we must have been! Glad that my new rollator had large wheels to deal with the changes in terrain. What fascinated me was that these five friends were more accommodating to me and the situation than my scholarly graduate school was! They somehow understood the situation after observing me for a few days, and they quickly ascertained my needs. Not everyone understands the squishy, confusing parts of MS – including me- – however, this little excursion was innovative and cleverly executed. It would have been very easy to leave me out of it entirely.

We all returned from that hike weary, especially my girlfriends. After all, each one of them had pushed my rollator, trying to converse and keep me as shaded as possible. My slurred speech was noticeable if I got too hot. So we all went back to the house for an evening of great food and conversation and a dip in the pool. I took breaks and rested between activities.

The next day we went to my friend's family lake house. This was slightly more than an hour from Apex. Heather drove and I was the comfortable passenger watching; there was little room for error, since we followed the other cars.

What a beautiful sight the lake house was, perched on a small hill with Gaston Lake below and several other houses scattered around the lake. I made a wise decision on the first day to stay in the air-conditioning and enjoy the view of the lake from the large porch. The heat and humidity would have ruined my day. The lake house was so joyful with a group of girlfriends enjoying one each other's company. We cooked, ate wonderful meals, danced, told stories and just had fun. I danced too, with someone always holding on to me or swinging my arms to different songs! I have always wanted to dance but had given up on that thought over the years. This was so empowering. To think I would swim and dance again, have fun again!

After this trip, which lasted about a week, I returned home. I was happy to be home. My home is special and has come a long way since the early days when I visited David for the first time. I have added my own touches and together we have made this "our" home. Home is what I felt I never had and now I do.

The experience with my girlfriends made me feel like a whole person again. I think about how I probably would be just like them if things had turned out differently, but there was no time to think that way. And then I had a home and David to come back to!

SOME THOUGHTS

• •

I am honored to feel as though I actually have some important thoughts about my life! From the day of diagnosis, life has evolved in the most challenging and empowering way. No doubt there were some unfair and sad times during this evolution, but thanks to the human spirit, I prevailed. I never realized that multiple sclerosis meant a lifelong relationship. Yes, it certainly is, but the volume of its intensity can be turned down. The high intensity and pressure seems to remain for many years with struggling and asking the same questions year after year. I am sure others with the same diagnosis will agree. I am not sure what begins the healing process. In my case, I had started writing down my thoughts many years ago, but it wasn't until recently, after my road trip to North Carolina, that I started feeling inspired enough to get my writing published. This showed me that healing had definitely begun a few years before the trip, and my going to be with friends was without question the catalyst that confirmed that I was indeed ready to live in acceptance.

We all have hardships that can plague us and we all have our own ways of coping. I refer to all the tragedies in the anxious world now. But I used all the lessons provided to me in various forms including education, friendships, love and just life to learn about myself. Having felt the unconditional love of friends and even strangers, I am humbled by the ways we all connect. One is never alone, and I despair that some people feel that way. I have always said, "I want to be the kind of person I want to be around." The universe will give back to one who is hurting, never give up! I am the author and advocate of my own life, and I must never forget that.

In peace, love and good health, I wish you the very best in life.

Printed in the United States
By Bookmasters